LANCASTER
at WAR

This was the noblest aircraft of them all.
Its flying qualities were gentle, and the
design factors so combined, that all its
crews could stand up and say
THIS was the Lancaster.

BILL SPOWAGE
(with apologies to Shakespeare)

LANCASTER at WAR

MIKE GARBETT and BRIAN GOULDING

LONDON

IAN ALLAN LTD

To those
who gave their all

First published 1971
Ninth impression 1983

ISBN 0 7110 0225 8

Published by Ian Allan Ltd, Shepperton,
Surrey; and printed in the United Kingdom
by Clark Constable (1982) Ltd, Edinburgh

Contents

Photo credits

The photographs in this book have been provided by:

A & AEE Official 11 (foot)
T. F. W. Addis 107 (upper right)
The Aeroplane 126 (upper)
K. Alefounder 144 (upper)
H. Allen 65 (upper), 98 (upper), 113 (foot), 123 (centre right)
N. W. Atkin 44
Australian War Memorial 46
The authors 137 (top, centre)
S. Baker 103 (lower), 124 (top right)
J. P. Bannister 55 (lower right)
P. D. Baxter 65 (lower)
D. S. Beckwith 77 (top)
P. C. Birch 120 (upper centre)
R. Bradley 89 (upper left)
W. Bradley 84 (upper)
D. B. Bretherton 77 (foot)
R. N. Brisley 120 (upper right)
E. A. Brookes 86 (upper)
R. J. Broome 120 (lower right)
Charles E. Brown 8, 18, 72
F. G. Brownings 112 (top)
L. Bustock 119 (foot)
G. F. Cadd 123 (centre left)
Canadian Armed Forces 27 (lower), 28, 37 (lower), 39 (lower), 42 (foot), 59 (upper), 62, 63 (second from top), 68, 70 (upper), 85 (lower), 119 (top right), 121 (lower), 133 (top, centre)
Canadian National Museum of Science and Technology 132, 133 (foot), 134 (lower)
D. B. Cassell 78 (centre), 86 (lower)
M. J. Cawsey 142, 143
Central Press Photos Ltd. 19, 34 (lower right), 63 (top, foot), 69 (upper), 122
Cliff C. Chatten 73 (centre)
J. Chatterton 131 (foot)
P. J. Coffey 93, 106
S. P. Daniels 136
Daily Express 13 (lower), 127 (upper)
R. A. Denny 138 (upper)
E. Dickinson 112 (foot)
Ted Eley 94
G. H. Everitt 114 (upper)
John Farrar 125 (foot)
R. C. Fentiman 123 (foot)
Fox Photos Ltd. 14, 34 (upper), 47 (left), 49 (centre), 50, 102 (lower), 103 (upper), 112 (centre), 115, 116
R. G. Funnell 104 (lower)
Mrs. E. Gill 109 (foot)
J. E. Goldsmith 118 (second from top)
Bill Goodwin 85 (upper)
GPU/Thomson Newspapers 101 (upper)
H. H. Grant-Dalton 108 (top, centre)
L. H. Gregson 27 (upper)
J. S. Griffiths 124 (centre)
J. Grimsy 40
F. H. Harper 141 (lower)
L. G. A. Hadland 23
B. R. W. Hallows 104 (upper right), 114 (lower)
R. J. Harris 107 (lower)
S. J. Harrison 123 (top)

D. W. Haseldine 83
F. C. Hopcroft 120 (lower left)
H. R. Humphries 21, 76, 113 (top, centre)
J. C. Hutcheson 124 (top left)
Imperial War Museum 29 (upper left, upper right), 31, 32, 37 (upper), 48 (lower), 56 (upper), 63 (third from top), 73 (foot), 77 (centre), 78 (top, foot), 79, 80, 81, 82, 102 (upper), 109 (top, centre), 124 (centre, foot), 129
A. C. Jack 11 (top)
O. A. K. Jones 73 (top)
Keystone 111 (foot)
P. V. Knights 118 (foot), 119 (top left)
J. O. Lancaster 33 (upper)
J. Lee 51 (upper left)
H. W. Lees 107 (upper left)
Lincolnshire Echo 138 (lower)
A. McCartney 54 (upper), 137 (foot)
N. R. McCorkindale 118 (top)
R. McIlwaine 121 (upper left)
E. H. Manners 30
P. L. Morgan 131 (top)
E. Morrey 42 (top)
P. J. R. Moyes 134 (upper)
Official 34 (lower left), 90, 141 (upper)
L. J. S. O'Hanlon 120 (upper left)
N. D. Owen 38 (lower)
B. Pape 38 (upper)
B. G. Payne 29 (lower)
Photopress Ltd. 55 (upper)
Planet News – United Press International 101 (lower)
RAAF Official 97, 121 (upper right), 127 (lower)
Radio Times Hulton Picture Library 17, 36 (lower), 51 (upper right, lower), 52 (upper, lower left), 53, 54 (lower), 57, 58 (upper), 59 (lower), 60, 70 (lower), 71, 111 (centre)
W. Reid 110
D. Reiner 55 (lower left)
D. S. Richardson 131 (centre)
A. V. Roe 13 (upper), 56 (lower), 135 (upper, lower)
Rolls-Royce Ltd. 11
Royal Netherlands Air Force via G. J. Zwanenburg 144 (lower)
D. A. Shaw 58 (lower)
C. Smith 126 (lower)
J. Smith 108 (foot)
R. J. Souter 84 (lower)
The Sun/People 104 (upper left)
Syndication International (Odhams) 12, 15, 20, 24, 25, 26, 36 (upper), 47 (right), 48 (upper), 49 (top, foot), 64
K. Talbot 39 (upper)
P. F. Thompson 118 (third from top)
Thomson Newspapers Ltd. 33 (lower), 61, 98 (lower), 125 (top)
Topical Press 117
J. R. Tuckwell 42 (centre)
R. Valentine 95
R. G. Walker 69 (lower)
J. Walsh 52 (lower right)
R. S. Webb 43 (upper)
D. West 43 (lower), 128
N. Westby 111 (top)
F. D. Wolfson 130 (lower)
R. G. Woodin 119 (centre)
G. J. Zwanenburg 89 (upper right, lower), 130 (upper)

Foreword

by Marshal of the Royal Air Force
SIR ARTHUR T. HARRIS, Bt
GCB, OBE, AFC, LLD
Air Officer Commanding-in-Chief, Bomber Command
February 1942 – September 1945

This remarkable book is a well-deserved tribute to a remarkable aircraft and to those who designed and built her – Roy Chadwick, A. V. Roe's Chief Designer, Roy Dobson, Managing Director, and the thousands of men and women who laboured with skill and devotion to put that Shining Sword into the hands of Bomber Command crews.

The Lancaster, beyond doubt, was a major factor in beating the Nazi enemy down to defeat – as even the enemy admitted. But no aircraft, however outstanding its qualities, can be an effective weapon of war unless the aircrew that man them are also of superlative quality. That the Lancaster crews were of such a breed is evidenced by the deeds and experiences related in this book.

This country, and its allies, owe these young men – the Many that died, the Few that survived – a debt they have not met: because it can never be met in full.

It is due to them, and their kind in the other Services, that Britain today is not a mere slave market in a Nazi Empire. That was the Plan.

Never forget it.

Arthur T. Harris

Introduction

It is now over a quarter of a century since the Lancaster last flew operationally during World War II; fifteen years have elapsed since its withdrawal from the RAF in 1956, and the last users, the Royal Canadian Air Force, the French Navy and the Argentine Air Force, retired their Lancasters in 1963/4. Yet the magic of the name 'Lancaster' remains, and still there is the strongest feeling of affection for this great aircraft, 'the old Lanc', as it became so widely known. If the name Spitfire became synonymous with saving the war for Britain, so the name Lancaster became synonymous with the winning of it.

For eighteen years the Lancaster has occupied a great deal of both our lives. Neither of us was old enough to have served on them, and we cannot put our finger on what it was that sparked our interest in the Lancaster in preference to other fine aircraft. Was it the Lancaster's looks, its performance, its sound or achievements? It is impossible to say, but something about it set us off on a trail of research that has taken us thousands of miles, and brought us into contact with hundreds of nice people all over the world who were either directly connected with the Lancaster or who share our interest in it.

Our efforts have been truly a labour of love, which has cost us dearly in time and money. What started as a schoolboy interest when the Lancaster was ending its front-line RAF life has blossomed into more than a hobby, rather a way of life, which has snowballed so rapidly in recent years that it has become impossible to 'get off', not that either of us would care to do so.

This is our third book on the Lanc and in it we have endeavoured to depict the aircraft in the wartime environment for which it was designed. We trust the many who operated in them post-war – including the Canadians, French and Argentinians – will forgive their omission on this occasion. They are by no means forgotten and their stories will be told in time.

In the preparation of this book, recourse to official records has been minimal. We have, over the years, searched the files of the Imperial War Museum, Air Ministry, Defence Ministry, etc., and spent many hours in the archives of the news agencies, uncovering dusty boxes of wartime prints which had lain forgotten for years.

Some of the photographs have been published before, but in most cases, during the war on poor quality magazine paper. In this book we hope they are done full justice.

It is those photographs reproduced from private sources which, we feel, convey the true atmosphere of Lancaster operations; not the official, posed, censored shots, but those taken – albeit illicitly – by the men who flew and maintained Lancasters. Although photography was, in general, strictly prohibited until the last few months of the war, when senior squadron pilots were allowed cameras, we have nevertheless acquired several thousand prints of Lancasters and crews from men who risked a snapshot of their beloved machine; men determined to record their part in the war effort. The developing and printing of their film by 'a friend in the photographic section' would cost them dearly in bribes of cigarettes or sweets.

Somehow, thankfully, these pictures got taken despite the risks involved, and many such snapshots are used in this book. There are many more which we would like to have used, but space and quality are unavoidable constraints.

Because the British were so notoriously anti-camera during the war – perhaps understandably so in the earlier years – there are large gaps in our history. How we envy the historian writing of the Lancaster's American counterparts, the B17 Fortress and B24 Liberator, with a vast, seemingly inexhaustible supply of superb action photographs from which to choose, almost every aircraft in their daylight formations having one or more cameras aboard. We cannot match their formation pictures, their battle scenes, aircraft being hit by flak, crews baling out, combats, contrails, etc. It must also be remembered that the Lancaster operated mainly by night until the last year of the war, giving much less opportunity for photography.

Official British sources are relatively sparse. Many priceless photographs remain locked away in official archives, unavailable to the enthusiast, while thousands more are known to have been destroyed, regardless of historical significance. We would like to have shown more photographs of Lancasters downed in enemy territory; photographs which we have actually seen in official albums in London, acquired from the Germans. Unfortunately, some obscure rule can always be found to prevent these really priceless pictures being released.

And so we turned to the private sources – the ex-aircrew; the fitters, armourers, orderlies and clerks, even the WAAFs – the men who flew the Lancs and the men and women who kept them flying. It is to them that this book is wholeheartedly dedicated.

It is not possible to mention by name all those who have helped, but we extend our grateful thanks for the logbooks, photographs, diaries and other material which has so trustingly been loaned to us from all over the world. In particular we must mention the following, without whose help this book would not have been published: Chris Ashworth, Derek Monk and Ray Sturtivant, the other three members of our original 'Lancaster Syndicate'; Trevor Allen; Leslie Butson; Jack Gregson; Olive Hamilton; Harry Holmes (who we know will not mind being between two ladies); Lena Johnson; Ted Manners; Philip Moyes; Cyril Parrish; John Rawlings; Bruce Robertson, whose own Lancaster book will always remain the standard reference work on the subject; Bill Spowage; Ron Valentine; Rusty Waughman and Gerrie Zwanenburg.

Also we wish to thank: various members of *Air Britain*; the staff of Avro's, Woodford, including Jack Beatty, Derek Bowyer, Ken Foden, Bill Hannah, Sandy Jack; Jack Hilton and staff of Avro Canada; the Australian War Memorial; *Blackwood's Magazine*; Brigadier-General Bourgeois and the staff of the Canadian Armed Forces HQ; R. W. Bradford of the Canadian National Museum of Science & Technology (Aviation Division); Maurice Smith, the Editor, and staff of *Flight International*; J. F. R. Painter of Hawker Siddeley Canada Ltd.; the staff of the Imperial War Museum; L. A. Jacketts and staff of the MoD (Air Historical Branch); J. H. G. Bennett and staff of the MoD (Publicity 3); the staff of the Press Association and its photographic agencies; W. R. Collier of Rose Brothers; the Royal Australian Air Force.

The authors of the factual accounts and impressions deserve a special mention. We are grateful for having been allowed to publish such highly personal documents, most of which were written shortly after the events described. It was not always easy to persuade the authors to donate such features because of the old fear of being accused of 'line shooting'. Their individual styles have been faithfully preserved.

Our sincere thanks, therefore, to:

'Biff' Baker	Lt/Col Johnny Goldsmith, CAF
Bill Bennée	Ken Lane
Bill Breckenridge	Carl Olsson
Don Charlwood	'Blue' Rackley
Lance Connery	Capt Rod Rodley
Edward Cook	John Shelton
Jack Currie	Fred Smooker
Lettice Curtis	Stan Wells
Jimmy Griffiths	

MIKE GARBETT
BRIAN GOULDING

THE EARLY DAYS

THE START OF IT ALL *The prototype Manchester, out of which the Lancaster was born, photographed (above) at Ringway on July 24, 1939, the day of her first flight. The Manchester's engines proved unsatisfactory and the decision to replace the two Vultures with four Merlins was probably one of the most momentous of the war.*

FIRST OF THE MANY *The prototype Lancaster, BT308, clearly showing the triple fins (below), seen at Ringway in early January 1941, at about the time of her first flight. Only this machine had the three fins, all subsequent Lancasters having the enlarged twin fins and extended tailplane.*

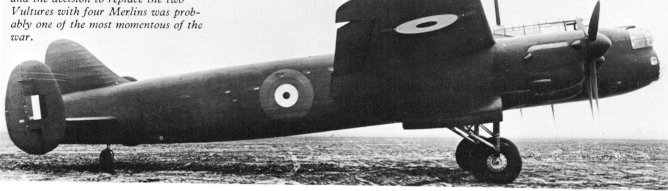

SHE CLIMBS LIKE A BIRD *The second prototype, DG595, in standard prototype camouflage, with yellow undersurfaces a sharp contrast to the standard bomber black, climbs away while on service trials at Boscombe Down. The ventral turret fitting is clearly seen, but it was not persevered with for long in squadron service, being of no use on night raids.*

IN PRODUCTION

THE BIRD TAKES SHAPE *Production line 1942. The scene at A. V. Roe's main plant at Chadderton, where the major manufacturing processes took place. Consisting of 55,000 separate parts, it has been estimated that half a million different manufacturing opera-* *tions were involved to produce just one aircraft.*

Peak production was achieved in August 1944 when the Lancaster Group as a whole turned out 293 machines, of which the Avro factories alone contributed 155.

HERE'S MY BODY – MY NOSE IS FOLLOWING *The Lancaster consisted of some 31 main components to permit dispersed production, and broke down into four sections for transport by road.*

A. V. Roe, the parent company, had several factories in the Manchester area which supplied components to the main plant at Chadderton. *The final marriage of wings, fuselage and tail took place at Woodford or Ringway, nearly 20 miles away, from where the completed machines would be test flown.*

This new BIII, ND824, *is seen on Greengate, outside the Chadderton factory before starting its journey to Woodford early in March 1944.*

FINAL ASSEMBLY *The huge assembly shed at Woodford, June 1942, where the major sections of the Avro and Metropolitan-Vickers-built Lancasters were finally married and the engines fitted.*

The shining sword

Jack Currie

Aircraft come and go, but few leave a lasting impression. One which attained true greatness was the Avro Lancaster.

Right from the start, A. V. Roe knew they had a winner. Watching the prototype take to the air for the first time, Sir Roy Dobson, managing director, turned to Roy Chadwick, chief designer, and said ecstatically, "Oh boy, oh boy . . . what an aeroplane! WHAT a piece of aeroplane!"

Of all the glowing tributes heaped on the immortal Lancaster, none can top that of Sir Arthur Harris, Chief of Bomber Command from 1942 to 1945. His eloquent words in his book, *Bomber Offensive*, are well known. Less known are his words in a letter to the Lancaster production group on its disbandment at the end of 1945.

"As the user of the Lancaster during the last three and a half years of bitter, unrelenting warfare, I would say this to those who placed that shining sword in our hands: 'Without your genius and your effort, we would not have prevailed – the Lancaster was the greatest single factor in winning the war.'"

Perfect in every way, a pilot's aeroplane without a single vice, the Lanc inspired confidence – evinced by the flight engineer who, having feathered two engines, pondered over the prospect of flying over several hundred miles of cold, unfriendly ocean. With deep gloom but perfect sincerity, he turned to his skipper and said, "I suppose this means we shall be bloody late for breakfast!"

Flying the Lancaster was mainly a man's prerogative, and the following impressions by Jack Currie would be echoed by most operational pilots. His enthusiasm is balanced by the views of a former ATA girl who found the Lancaster too much of a 'Gentleman's' aeroplane to test her flying skill. But then, perhaps her endearment had not been heightened by safe returns from ops!

I was a sergeant-pilot, twenty-one years old, flying Wellingtons at an operational training unit near Derby, when they told me I was going to fly Lancasters. There were two other types of heavy bomber in the command, the Halifax and the Stirling, but most people said the Lancaster was the best.

14

ROLL OUT *A. V. Roe alone employed around 40,000 people by 1943, the majority being engaged in Lancaster production. Women formed 44 per cent of the Lancaster labour force and here (facing page) a lady tractor driver tows out a brand new machine, fresh off the assembly line.*

CAREFUL, SHE'S NEW *Marshaller Walter Holland will be thinking as driver Alf Beacon brings a brand-new Lanc to the flight line after leaving the assembly sheds at Woodford. This BI, R5493, was destined to be the first Lancaster lost on operations – failing to return from a gardening sortie to Lorient on March 24, 1942.*

We finished OTU and went to Lincolnshire for heavy conversion. We did some flying in Halifaxes, and picked up a flight engineer and another gunner, which made up the crew to seven. There were some Lancasters belonging to the finishing school on the airfield, and I could hardly wait to get my hands on one of them. The Lancaster looked good because everything was well shaped and in proportion, and she had a good flying attitude. Some aeroplanes look as though they're leaning forward, and some look as though they're being pushed along from behind, but the Lancaster rode the air smoothly, easily and steadily.

You got into the Lancaster either through the main door at the back, or up a ladder into the nose. When you reached the cockpit it seemed a long way off the ground. The pilot's seat was comfortable and you could see around well. The cockpit smelled good. There was a long list of checks to go through before you could start the engines, then more checks before you got moving, and more before take-off.

It wasn't very easy to taxi along a narrow, winding track out to the runway. You turned by gunning the outer engine, and straightened up by giving the opposite outer engine a burst, but there was a lot of inertia, and you had to anticipate each turn. You had to keep a good grip on the brake lever, otherwise she would run away with you. A screened pilot sat next to me for the first take-off and landing. You opened the throttles with your right hand, palm down, leading with the thumb on the port outer to stop her swinging left. You pushed the stick forward to get the tail up as soon as you could, because then you could steer with the rudders instead of the engines.

For landing, you had to take the power right off on rounding out, or she would float on and on down the runway and never touch down. You had to remember these things on take-off and landing and get used to them. In between take-off and landing the Lanc flew herself. She was a dream aeroplane.

All the crew were happy about the Lanc and their own bit of her. The bomb aimer was down in the nose with the bombsight and release gear, and he could also man the front gun-turret. Up a step behind him you came to the cabin, where I sat on the left and the flight engineer on the right. If you wanted to get past the flight engineer, from the cabin into the nose, he had to push his foot-rest out of the way and swing his feet up, and then you could crawl under his seat. The navigator sat at a little desk behind me, facing left, with the wireless operator aft of him. The navigator could take sextant shots through the astrodome above the wireless op's right shoulder. Back down the fuselage aft of the cabin, you passed the rest-bed and came to the mid-upper gun-turret sticking out of the roof. You squeezed past that to get to the main door and the Elsan closet, and finally to the rear turret, poking out at the back between the rudders.

We heard a lot of stories about casualties on the squadrons, how this or that crew had 'got the chop', people we had been training with at OTU or HCU. Some squadrons were supposed to have better luck than others, or better leadership or maintenance. I felt confident of the Lancaster and of the crew, and I didn't pay much attention to these stories.

With full petrol tanks and a normal bombload, the Lancaster climbed slowly. You were briefed to bomb from 20,000 feet, give or take a thousand feet or so, but the last few thousand were hard to reach, especially on a warm night. On a short-range target like the Ruhr, you couldn't reach 20,000 feet by the time you got to the target even if you climbed hard all the way. So you had to climb the first 10,000 feet or so over base before setting course. The idea of hundreds of bombers circling around together over Lincolnshire was a bit fearsome, especially in cloud. One evening I saw two Lancasters collide at about 10,000 feet and they both blew up.

Once you levelled out, she settled down nicely to a steady 150 mph indicated or a bit more, and she was manoeuvrable with the full load on. There was a constant volume of noise all the time. You couldn't hear anything that was going on outside the aircraft, like thunder or flak-bursts or other aircraft, unless they were very close. You did hear anything that hit you, even rain or sleet, and hail sounded very loud on the canopy. You could usually hear your own guns when they fired, and you could feel them make the aircraft throb. Over a hot target I sometimes let my seat right down, so that I could concentrate on the bombing run without being put off by all the lights and flashes.

You could tell when the bomb doors were open by the change in the noise of the slipstream. When the bomb aimer let the bombs go, the Lancaster gave a little jump.

I listened to the engines all the time. The flight engineer tried to get all four going at the same rpm with the propeller-pitch levers, and then I fiddled with them to get the sound exactly right. If there was any sort of light you could synchronise the engines by getting the shadows on the propellers all at the same angle. On the way home from a long-range target I sometimes fell asleep for a second, and immediately woke up in a cold sweat because I couldn't hear the engines in my sleep, and thought they had stopped.

The Lanc always did everything I asked her to do, and some things I couldn't reasonably have expected. Once we flew home with both ailerons broken clean off at the hinges. We got through a searchlight cone and some flak over Heligoland, crossed the North Sea and made a reasonable landing at base. I steered her with the rudders and outer engines. I told the crew it might be a good idea to bale out, but they all had enough confidence to stay on board.

Another time both port engines were out, with one propeller feathered and the other windmilling, and we had to make an emergency landing in Kent. There was an enemy raid going on, and most of the aerodrome lights were out. I misjudged the approach and had to go round again. We'd got the wheels and some of the flap down, part of the bombload still on board, and hardly enough height to try it. Going round again on two engines on the same side was never a good idea, but she made it.

Sometimes the airspeed indicator used to get iced up, and then it didn't give a true reading. It usually came unstuck once you got down below the freezing level, but once it didn't, and we had to land with it like that. The rear gunner said he could tell whether we were fast or slow on the approach by the noise of the slipstream around his turret. He was right too, because we made a better landing than usual.

You could really throw the Lanc around if you wanted to. We used to have practice scraps with the Spitfire boys, and if the gunners knew their stuff and gave you the word to go into the corkscrew at just the right moment, you could make it very difficult for the fighter to get a good shot in. Meanwhile the gunners were supposed to be shooting pieces out of the fighter. We played this game in earnest coming back from the Peenemunde raid on a bright moonlit night. A pair of Messerschmitts attacked us for ten minutes, but we got away with it, and the mid-upper gunner knocked one of them down. I was warmly dressed for a long cold trip, and the exercise and the fright made me sweat like a horse.

I always called the Lancaster the Queen of the Sky, except when she floated a few feet off the ground on and on down the runway and didn't want to land. Then I used to say, "get down, you big black bastard", but the crew would make me take that back.

FAITH IN HIS OWN DESIGN
Roy Chadwick, the Lancaster's designer, on a test flight from Woodford in 1942. With A. V. Roe since World War I, he was to be tragically killed on August 23, 1947, in a Tudor, together with the company's chief test pilot, Bill Thorne, who is seen at the controls in this picture. Also in the flight test crew are Donald Woods (foreground), Harry Barnes (with beret) and Syd Gleave (bending). At the peak of Lancaster production Avro's maintained seven full-time flight test crews (pilot and flight engineer) at Woodford, test- and production-flying being a continuous dawn-to-dusk task, every day of the week.

FIRST FLIGHT *A late production BI, PP687, on a test flight from Vickers Armstrong's Castle Bromwich factory in March 1945.*

Known as the Lancaster Group, companies building the Lancaster comprised A. V. Roe (Manchester area and Yeadon), Metropolitan-Vickers (Manchester area), Armstrong Whitworth (Baginton), Vickers-Armstrong (Chester and Castle Bromwich), Austin Motors (Longbridge) and Victory Aircraft Canada (Malton).

Masking tape clearly shows the fuselage sections. The painting of the aircraft would be completed at either an RAF Maintenance Unit or on the Squadrons, where codes would be added.

ROUND THE CLOCK *As evening approaches work continues at the factories; a scene at Woodford in September 1943, as yet another new Lanc is prepared for the next day's flight, the tractor manned by two ladies, Joan Brough and Freda Turner.*

... and the woman's view

Miss Lettice Curtis

The Lancaster was by far the easiest of the wartime heavy bombers to fly and, as such, was not used for four-engined training in ATA. I am sure that any competent twin-engine pilot could have got into a Lancaster and flown it without any trouble.

Although up to 1943 some ATA pilots were trained on the Stirling, the majority graduated on the Halifax and in fact, after spring 1943, all training took place at Marston Moor where an ATA Halifax training flight was run in conjunction with the RAF.

Unlike singles and twins, each four-engined aircraft was endorsed on one's authorisation card separately. After ferrying ten of the type on which one had been trained, one progressed to further types by doing two trips in the right-hand seat, and one ferry trip with another pilot to see – literally, because there was no question of any dual – what went on. Then one went out and ferried one oneself. The Lanc was so straightforward it was the only aircraft on which we did not have to do these 'stooge' trips.

I was lucky enough to be the first woman to be cleared four-engines in February 1943. I flew my first Lanc in April, ED396, from Llandow to Elsham Wolds. In May 1943 I delivered ED817/G from Farnborough to Scampton, then a grass airfield. Although I suppose we knew about the dam busting we had no idea where the dam busters were based and so I had no reason to know that this was a specially modified aircraft. We flew quite a lot of /G aircraft, mostly Halifaxes fitted with H2S for the Pathfinders and Coastal Command; and, incidentally, a friend used to tell me that Bomber Command had to release the Halifax to Coastal not only because of the ASV MkII, but because the Lancs had very poor ditching characteristics. They sank in minutes if they came down in the sea.

I used to get a tremendous satisfaction from landing a Lib or from three-pointing a Stirling or a Halifax, but the Lanc was a straightforward, safe and efficient but, I fear, a rather dull and characterless flying machine!

Miss Curtis delivered several hundred aircraft while serving with the Air Transport Auxiliary.

UNUSUAL ANGLE *on Avro test pilots Sam Brown and Bill Thorne as they prepare to enter one of the early production Lancs at Woodford in the spring of 1942.*

ENTRY INTO SERVICE

THE NEW WEAPON ENTERS SERVICE *To No. 44 (Rhodesia) Squadron fell the honour of introducing the Lancaster in squadron service; the first three being delivered on Christmas Eve 1941 – a welcome present for the Squadron whose ageing Hampdens had done sterling work but had now become outmoded. BI, L7537, KM-L, the first machine to be delivered to a Squadron.*

The tip-off

Rod Rodley

Flying a new type of aircraft is always hazardous, in wartime particularly, when new types had to be rushed into service to meet a pressing need. The Lanc, beautiful flying machine though she was, had her share of teething troubles. Never before had a bomber been asked to carry so much at so great a speed, and in the early days it was a journey into the unknown for crews and designers alike.

Some crews got away with it – many didn't. Those who did were able to contribute vital information which, pieced together, helped to make the Lanc the best bomber and one of the safest flying machines of World War II.

This story, told by Rod Rodley, who was later to survive the Augsburg raid and who still flies airliners today, shows how, by a cool piece of flying and a certain amount of good fortune, he was able to provide vital evidence of some structural weakness at an early stage, which resulted in the whole of the Lancaster force being temporarily grounded.

The operation was 97 Squadron's first with the Lancaster, only seventeen days after 44 Squadron had pioneered the first operation on Lancs.

The squadron had only had Lancasters for a couple of

months, and bombloads and fuel loads were worked out somewhere above my level in the hierarchy so, when a low-level attack on Essen was cancelled one morning because of dwindling cloud, I was very happy. Group, however, thought we should do some training and we were tanked up for a long cross-country, despite the fact that a front was giving a cloud base of 300–400 feet and visibility of half a mile in rain. (We lost three or four Lancs that day landing around the countryside.)

Suddenly, it was all changed. "Go and lay some mines along the Frisian Islands." So, six 1,500lb sea-mines were loaded by the cursing armourers, a total load, with our 2,154 gallons of fuel, well above maximum take-off weight! Not that I knew anything about that!

Poor old L7570 OF-B took off from a soaking Wood-hall somewhere about lunchtime, and I decided to stay under the low cloud to get an accurate fix as we crossed the coast, so that we would not go blundering into the defences on the other side of the sea. I was at about 350 feet when I saw houses and a cemetery come into view, and realised I was too far north and this was Boston, with its Stump* higher than we were! I im-

* St. Botolph's Church Tower.

mediately turned right and at that moment ran into some low wrack. As this cleared, I was horrified to see the ground coming up at a steep angle. I eased her up as gently as possible, not wanting to stall into the town, and we roared across the rooftops, damaging some property with our aerial-weight, which was swinging about only 35 feet below us.

Chiding myself for an atrocious turn, I climbed gingerly away, hoping no one had got my number, when my Canadian co-pilot, 'Junior' Colquhoun, turned a pale face to me and said, "Holy Jeez, Rod, d'you know your wingtips are missing?"

I looked out and on the starboard side there was just a bright jagged aluminium line where the tip used to be. On the port side, a six-foot high green and sand tip of camouflage paint stood at right angles to the wing. I noticed too that the far end of the aileron abutted on to this, and realised the danger of nipping the aileron if I slipped in on a turn.

I was frozen with horror; seven bods in a kite full of 100 octane and six mines, flying in atrocious weather and nowhere to go! I certainly couldn't fling this Lanc about trying to make a bad weather circuit. Just then we crossed the coast and I saw a beautiful flat expanse of sand, ample for my purpose, so I decided to put her down. I turned gingerly, called the crew up to crash positions and eased back the throttles.

With the wheels retracted, I flew lower and lower over the sand until I felt the tailwheel running along. Gently back with the stick as we lost speed, and then the inner props struck and we were down. We bucketed along for a couple of hundred yards and I was aware of a thumping and rolling underneath – I realised later it was the cylindrical mines – and suddenly all was quiet except for the loud crackling and tinkling of cooling engines. I pressed the fire-extinguisher for good luck and turned to crack a joke, only to find I was alone!

I opened the side window, put my head out into the rain and saw six figures disappearing into the mist. I bellowed at them to come back and they shouted to me, "Leave it, it's going to go up." We compromised and met halfway.

Opening our escape outfits, we got out our 1-in. diameter compasses and decided to strike north-west into the rain and mist to ensure we hit the coast somewhere. The sandbanks were intersected by deep runnels in which water was flowing strongly westwards, so we guessed that the tide was making. Our Sidcots and flying boots didn't help. One of us left a boot in deep mud, but we hurried on, treading carefully over all sticks because we had been warned of anti-invasion mines. My chief regret at the time was that I couldn't get the Lanc salvaged before the sea came up. She seemed undamaged except for the bomb doors she had landed on, plus the bent props.

Suddenly Merralls, my wireless op, remembered his pigeon, so we had to wait while he retraced his steps to rescue the bird.

On we went, shouting every now and then, but only the ripple of the tide and the odd sea bird answered. Then we heard running feet, labouring breath, and out of the murk appeared a Home Guard. We were saved! But, he ran past us. I shouted to him and he briefly looked at us and said, "Straight on the way you're going. Turn left at the path. I'm going to look at the crash."

We guessed it was the clock he was going to look at but pressed on, feeling rather happier, if less heroic.

We found the path, turned left and came to a pub. There we were received rather casually as we stamped in, wet and muddy, and flung our parachutes down. "Was it you just went over?" We confirmed this and then rum was produced and sunk for purely medicinal purposes and to ward off the evil eye. I needed it too, because many evil eyes were on me for a few weeks after that.

The Group Engineer Officer was good enough to doubt my word and was convinced I had deliberately low-flown and knocked my wingtips off on the roofs. However, the tips were produced, one from Boston and one from the wreck, which disproved this uncharitable theory. I was pleased to note that Air Marshal John Slessor kept a very open mind during this period.

A little while later, the squadron was visited by a high-powered committee, and to my surprise I was called to the watch office where a civilian asked me to walk on the grass with him. He introduced himself as Roy Chadwick, Avro's chief designer. He explained that Britain had sunk everything into the Lanc and he *had* to know if my story was true. He said that if I had been larking about (*sic*!) it would go no further and that production could go on. On assuring him of my veracity, he accepted it and I believe production was halted, and a campaign commenced on all the Lancs then flying. Fortunately for me, they found a weakness in the tip attachment and I was exonerated. The necessary modifications were quickly put in hand and the Lanc got into its stride once again.

That was that, except that my rear gunner had an injured foot, received when he finished up at a 'bit of a run' as we touched down before he had reached his crash position. That was Jack Crisp, now a famous modern painter.

I believe a gallant armaments officer went to the wreck later, cut a hole and crawled in to de-fuse the mines which had been made live and magnetically dangerous by the act of the sea dissolving their salt plugs.

L7578 *KM-B, flies low over Waddington, the first Lancaster station. The
latter view shows clearly the layout of
a typical pre-war airfield. This photograph was taken on one of 44 Squadron's
low-level formation practices carried out
in the week before the Augsburg raid in
April 1942, KM-B being flown at the*
*time by S/Ldr John Nettleton and his
co-pilot P/O Pat Dorehill, both
Rhodesians. For some reason she was
transferred to 97 Squadron only two
days before the raid actually took place,
Nettleton and crew taking over a
brand-new KM-B, R5508.*

PANORAMA OF POWER

STATION TURN OUT *With 21 Lancs in the background, sixteen crews of 12 and 626 Squadrons pose for a publicity-cum-propaganda shot on a cold and dismal day in January 1944 before setting off on yet another raid on the German capital. There is a story behind this picture. The press that day, January 20, were visiting Ludford Magna to see the workings of a bomber station and the preparations behind an operation. As the airfield housed 101 Squadron, censorship forbade publication of pictures showing the three aerials jutting from the fuselage of their special Lancs, so nearby Wickenby paraded its aircraft and crews to complete the pressmen's day. These pictures give some idea of what was involved in putting out a 'maximum effort' on one squadron alone.*

25

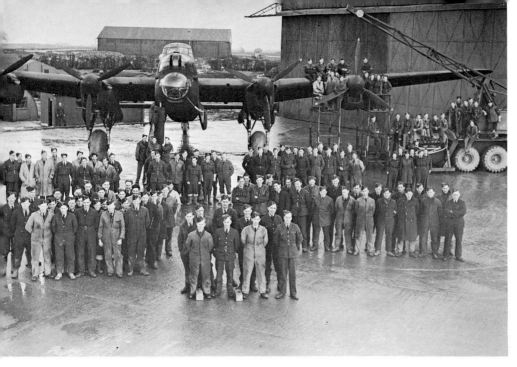

Not often did the men behind the scenes get into the picture. Here are some of those responsible for keeping the Lancasters flying. The Lanc in the background has somehow escaped the attention of the censor, though an attempt has been made to cover the nose aerial.

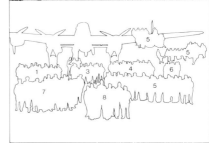

1. W/Os and NCOs.   2. Armourers.
3. W/T mechanics.   4. Electricians and instrument fitters.   5. Engine fitters.   6. Spark plug testers.   7. Airframe fitters.   8. Radio mechs.

Bomb load and handling crews for sending twenty Lancs to Berlin.

Some of the crews manning the petrol and oil bowsers, fire tenders, oxygen cylinders, etc.

MAKING READY

PLUG TROUBLE *A slight problem is sorted out on the starboard inner Merlin of a 622 Squadron Lanc BIII, LM511 GI-C, at Mildenhall in the summer of 1944.*

This example is a Packard-Merlin, built in the USA under licence. Ground crews particularly liked the magnificent toolkits supplied with the American-built engines.

PROP CHANGE *Changing the propellers of a Lanc was a delicate task as they each weighed around 500lb and had to be very finely balanced.*

Here, ground crew of 426 'Thunderbird' Squadron RCAF at Linton-on-Ouse show how it is done, with the aid of a special rig, while another 'erk' paints a motif on the nose. Under the letter K on the nose is painted — · — ('dah – di – dah', the letter in morse).

ENGINE SNAG *The ground crew of* KB762 *VR-J, a veteran MkX belonging to 419 'Moose' Squadron RCAF, discuss a problem with the starboard inner CSU, while two others remove the top panel. It is spring 1945 and the village church provides a sober contrast to an instrument of war at this Middleton St George dispersal.*

WHEEL CHANGE *This picture, taken at Linton-on-Ouse in 1943, gives some idea of the size of a Lancaster's main wheel and tyre assembly. No tread was deemed necessary at the time.*

In the background is a Lancaster II, DS741, *OW-T of the RCAF's 426 'Thunderbird' Squadron.*

GETTING GUNNED UP *Armourers slot in the four Browning .303s through the doors of the rear turret. The guns could fire a total of 1,200 rounds a minute, and although some Lancasters were later fitted with guns of .5 calibre, the .303s remained generally standard and were able to give a good account of themselves.*

IN GOES THE 'AMMO' *Feeding up .303 ammunition belts into the nose of a 617 Squadron BI, ED763 KC-Z, at Woodhall Spa in 1944. Capacity was 14,000 rounds, including reserves.*

This view shows clearly the Stabilised Automatic Bomb Sight (SABS) used only by 617.

BOOTS *Precariously poised, a ground crew bod struggles to release the cover from the front turret of a 115 Squadron Lanc BIII, ND758 A4-A, at Witchford, July 1944. The pilot's open window reveals the control locks still in place. Behind the wheel can be seen the ignition switches. The DV (direct vision) panel on the front corner of the cockpit is also open. Below the bomb motif is the later-style pitot head for the air speed indicator. Skipper of this kite was F/O Don S. McKechnie, RCAF.*

SECRET SERVICE *A hive of activity at 'Oor Wullie's' dispersal (BI, LL757), Ludford Magna, May 1944. Two masts on top of the fuselage, plus one under the nose (and barely visible here) signify No. 101 – a squadron with a difference. From October 1943 its Lancasters were fitted with special radio-jamming equipment known as ABC, or 'Airborne Cigar' and carried an eighth crew-member known as the 'Special Duties Operator'.*

'Airborne Cigar' was a development of 'Ground Cigar', used by special ground signals units to jam German *fighter broadcasts, but whose range was limited to a narrow band along the French and Dutch coasts.*

'Airborne Cigar' consisted of a receiver and three transmitters (hence the three aerials), a table with lamp, clock, etc., and was situated on top of the bomb bay aft of the main spar on the port side. The jamming signal was an undulating, warbling, almost musical note. The receiver included a cathode ray tube which gave a visual indication of every signal within the waveband covered. As soon as a signal appeared the special operator tuned his receiver *to it, and, having identified it, one of the transmitters would be tuned to the same frequency and switched on. He would then continue to search the band for other signals.*

In the early days the SDOs transmitted in German but the Germans soon overcame this by broadcasting on several wavelengths. This earlier method went under the code name 'Corona', but after it was discontinued, the SDOs simply searched for – and jammed – the messages etc. Because 101 was such a top-secret unit, this photograph had to be taken from inside a ground crew hut.

WINTER COATS *Early morning at Waddington, January 1945, with two Lancs looking cold and forlorn after an overnight fall of snow. Seldom would the snow, however heavy, hold up operations for more than a night or two. It was 'all hands to the brooms and shovels' with every available man and woman on the station lending a hand to clear runways, taxiways and dispersals.*

Air and ground crews of 630 squadron hard at it, in January 1945, at East Kirkby.

BOMBING UP

'JOE LANC' *Few men could say they flew their namesake. F/Lt 'Joe' Lancaster of 12 Squadron was one who could. Here he sits astride a dark green 'cookie' with cans of incendiaries behind, before loading into his faithful kite 'R-Robert' (BI, W4366 PH-R) at Wickenby in March 1943.*

HANDLE WITH CARE *Fitting the fins to 500-pounders at Skellingthorpe in August 1944. The bombs are a mixture of British and American, the latter distinguishable by their two shackle-rings.*

CHANGE HERE FOR CALAIS

These 115 Squadron armourers hitch a ride on the bomb trolleys out to a dispersal at Witchford on a summer day in 1944. The job of fusing and loading bombs was a dangerous, exacting one, which had to be accomplished no matter what the weather or time of day or night.

SAFELY STORED 1 *A typical area bombing load (below) – a 4,000lb 'cookie' surrounded by incendiaries in the bomb bay of an 83 Squadron Lanc at Scampton in June 1942.*

Of all the bombs dropped by Bomber Command, Lancasters dropped 63.8 per cent, amounting to 608,612 tons. Some 51,513,106 incendiaries were dropped.

SAFELY STORED 2 *A typical tactical target load (right). A 'cookie' and 500-pounders in the bay of the veteran BI, R5868 PO-S, at 467 Squadron, Waddington, in May 1944, destined for a marshalling yard in France.*

Twenty Lancasters

Carl Olsson

"RAF drops 1,500 tons on Duisburg . . ." "2,300 tons cascade on Hamburg . . ." so the newspaper headlines ran day after day.

To a great many people such headlines became just figures, a rough guide to the size and weight of a raid. Little did they realise what lay behind them – the nature of the toil, the cost and the prodigious human effort involved in reaching such plain tonnages of blast and flame.

A typical wartime airfield housed some 2,500 personnel, of which one-tenth comprised aircrew. It took dozens of men and women to send just one Lancaster on an operation. Not for them the glamour of flying and being in the public eye. Unheard and unseen to outsiders, theirs was a mundane routine job, but none-the less vital.

An aerodrome was a township, a factory, a battle headquarters and a front-line assault point from which men sallied forth to attack the enemy. It was never at complete rest. Throughout every twenty-four hours someone was working.

Set down among the fields of home, its 2,500 men and women led an entirely independent existence from the rest of the country for weeks on end. If they became ill or were injured, treatment would be in their own hospital. Canteens, kitchens and food stores, big enough to supply a small town, fed them. They had their own recreation facilities such as playing fields, cinema, sometimes even a dance hall, with a stage for variety shows.

In the maintenance stores was a vast array of spare parts, enough to refit completely about half of the aircraft on the station's strength.

Bomber Command will always be associated with the blasting of cities like Berlin, despite its tremendous onslaughts on tactical and industrial targets. An attack on the 'big city' in the winter of 1943/4 typifies a day in the life of a station.

Take-off would be before dusk, around 16.00 hrs, so that the long journey out and home would be completed before the moon rose, or early morning fog settled down on the aerodrome.

The day began before 08.00 with the handling crews hard at work in the bomb dump at the far end of the airfield. Scores of men slithered about in the mud, bringing 100lb cases of incendiaries to a central section where they were packed into the special containers known as SBCs.

They advanced from the dump in lines of ten, with the exception of the two end men, each holding in either hand one handle of the incendiary case. Thus, at each journey the men had to carry 900lb to the packing section.

In another part of the dump other men were rolling out the great 4,000lb 'cookies' and mounting them on low bomb trolleys. Others would be loading flares and leaflets. All this work went on without a pause or break till the early afternoon, when the trolleys were driven out to the aircraft. Lunch might be a hastily eaten sandwich and a mug of tea.

Meanwhile, in another section, armament crews were working against time, feeding tens of thousands of cartridges into the ammunition belts.

At the fuel dump the great Matador 2,500-gallon capacity petrol bowsers were being filled, and the 450-gallon oil bowsers also topped up. One petrol bowser held enough to fill one Lancaster for a long-distance journey, with a mere 300 gallons to spare. So many journeys had to be made back and forth from the storage tanks to the aircraft waiting at the dispersal pens that it would be mid-afternoon before all were filled.

At the dispersals ground crews were swarming over the kites in their charge. Every part had to be checked; engines, plugs, instruments, bomb door mechanism, and a host of other things. Some snag was nearly always found in one part or another of the aircraft and had to be set right, the toiling men always working against time.

If a fault connected with the flying ability was detected it had to be put right in time for a test flight, which had to be made to ensure the fault had been rectified long before take-off on the raid.

It sometimes happened that two or three test flights were made before the sweating ground crews completed the job to the satisfaction of the Captain of the aircraft. No aircrew liked flying in someone else's Lanc for, like cars, all had their own characteristics.

Over at the hangars two or three Lancs might be getting a special overhaul to put them into full serviceability at the hands of skilled maintenance fitters and riggers. Perhaps whole engines had to be changed, or a wing or tailplane, new instruments put in, or pipelines and cables refitted.

Test flights had to be made in these cases of course, and not infrequently the maintenance crews worked on the aircraft right up to a few minutes before take-off. There were cases of skilled crews refitting an engine less than an hour before take-off, which was certainly cutting it close.

While all this sweat and toil was going on at many different points of the airfield, other special staff also worked against time.

The Intelligence Officers were getting out data on the target, such as maps and photographs, collecting information from Group Headquarters and Path Finder

Force. All had to be ready for the briefing of the crews in the afternoon.

The Meteorological Officers collected and revised up to the minute weather information from their own central channels.

In the locker rooms, other staff sorted out all the items of clothing and equipment needed by each member of the aircrew as soon as briefing ended. About fifteen articles were required by each man, ranging from life-saving Mae Wests to socks.

In the kitchen, WAAFs cut sandwiches for nearly two hundred aircrew and parcelled up rations of chocolate, fruit, chewing gum and flasks of tea or coffee.

At Station Headquarters, the CO and his staff worked out the technical data for the trip ahead. Sometimes news came through from Group, making a change of plan necessary. It could happen that this change would result in most of the morning's work being altered within half an hour of briefing.

The only personnel who had no part in this unceasing labour were the aircrew. Theirs perhaps was the worst part – the waiting from the time they were 'warned' for a raid that night, until the final take-off. It was a long wait, broken only by the briefing and then by dressing up in the crew room.

But everyone else on the station doggedly carried on until the moment came when the last Lanc was signalled down the runway and off on the long trip ahead.

Then, and only then, did the tired ground crews, the bomb teams and the others stretch their aching limbs and take their ease in the canteens or mess halls. But not for long; in an hour or two it was time for bed, to be ready for an early morning start and another long, exhausting day.

VEGETABLES FOR EXPORT
Winching 1,500lb mines aboard a 106 Squadron kite at Syerston in November 1942. Each Lanc usually carried six.

From the first days of the war, Bomber Command waged a steady sea-mining campaign and of the Command's 18,725 'gardening' sorties, 2,929 were by Lancasters, on which a total of 12,733 mines was laid.

OPS ARE ON *While the armourers prepare the SBCs (small bomb containers) of incendiaries for loading, the undercarriage locks are removed. A scene at a 207 Squadron dispersal, Langar, in early May 1943.*

FUELLING

TOPPING UP – '2154 OF PETROL PLEASE' *The Matador bowser has been skilfully backed beneath the starboard engines of this 75 New Zealand Squadron Lanc, at rain-swept Mepal in January 1945. Even before the target was known, the petrol load gave crews some indication of the likely distance involved. If it was 2,154 gallons (the maximum) then it would mean a long stooge deep into enemy territory. Lancasters consumed some 228 million gallons of petrol in the course of operations.*

'. . . AND 150 OF OIL' *As a Hercules-engined MkII of a 6 Group RCAF squadron is topped up somewhere in East Yorkshire, autumn 1943.*

READY AT DISPERSAL

LINCOLNSHIRE SCENE 1 *A bleak landscape at Kirmington in the heart of the bomber country, home of 166 Squadron, with typically spartan ground-crew huts, the inevitable collection of squadron bikes and showing how widely the Lancasters were dispersed into the countryside, sometimes two or three miles from the main airfield buildings and hangars. The airfields covered large tracts of former agricultural land and were situated in some of the remotest parts of the country, often many miles from the nearest large town.*

LINCOLNSHIRE SCENE 2 *With a few precious minutes to spare before an air test, F/Lt Cliff Chatten, and part of his 97 Squadron crew, give some idea of the size of a Lanc. The pilot, standing on the far wing tip, will be nearly 100 feet away from the camera.*

In the background is Tattershall Castle, a landmark which became a very familiar sight to Coningsby crews.

LINCOLNSHIRE SCENE 3 *Up in the Lincolnshire Wolds, BI* NX560 *J-Jig² of 460 (Australian) Squadron stands quietly at dispersal on the perimeter of Binbrook in 1945.*

She has the round-ended props known as paddle blades, first introduced on the American-built Merlins, and later adopted as standard. They improved performance, particularly in the climb, and Lancs so fitted became commonly known as 'paddle steamers'. AR-J² is one of the rare BVII Interims.

RURAL SCENE *The farmhouse, the bare trees, the pale spring sunshine: a typically English backcloth, so well remembered by the thousands of Commonwealth airmen who had travelled to their mother country for the first time. Another scene at Middleton St George, Co. Durham. At dispersal is* KB882 *NA-R, a brand new Canadian-built BX of 428 "Ghost" Squadron. Behind the Lancaster is a protective earth blast-wall, a common sight beside far flung dispersal pans.*

THE UNSUNG HEROES

TEA-BREAK – 1944 STYLE
Smiles all around as the YMCA tea lady calls at a 617 Squadron dispersal, Woodhall Spa. The squadron dog seems to have lost all interest in the proceedings, as the lads have a 'cuppa tea and a wad'.

Women were rarely allowed at dispersal, as they were considered to be an unlucky omen. It is rumoured that some WAAFs actually had stones thrown at them by aircrew to keep them away from the aircraft!

Not all had wings

Stan Wells

On hearing I was posted to Wickenby, my first reaction was, "Where on earth is that?" No one seemed to know, but as I had been told that the squadron there had recently formed with Lancasters, it was presumably somewhere in Lincolnshire.

Having heard so much about the Lanc, I was pleased to be going to an operational squadron equipped with *the* premier weapon of Bomber Command. Word had spread that this aircraft had no vices, was a delight to fly, and what is more, was easy to service and maintain.

Poring over a map revealed a tiny village, from which the station derived its name, tucked away in the heart of rural Lincolnshire, about twelve miles from Lincoln and six from Market Rasen. Knowing a little of that county pre-war, I knew at least that the natives were a friendly lot!

Arriving on a typically cold and damp winter's day, my heart sank on seeing my new home. What a dump! Coming from a peacetime station, with permanent buildings, comfortable quarters and plenty of amenities, it was a shock to see the general drabness of the place. Ugly black steel-sheet hangars stood out like sore thumbs on the surrounding farmland. Concrete buildings with corrugated roofs and Nissen huts abounded, camouflaged and austere; purely functional.

At first sight there appeared to be no pattern at all, but on looking around the place, some thought had indeed gone into the layout. Hurriedly laid concrete paths led to each building and mud was everywhere.

However poor my first impressions were, I was to become very fond of Wickenby as the months rolled by. The dispersals were quite pleasantly situated, particularly those on the far side of the airfield, away from view and sheltered by trees. The latter were very welcome, especially when cold and bitter winds swept across the Wolds.

My Squadron, 626, had only recently formed from a flight of No. 12, a pre-war squadron, and with whom we were to share the 'drome until the end of the war.

The billets were situated some distance away and dispersed in case of air attack. Most were Nissen huts but made quite homely inside. In the centre of each was a round stove and it was a constant problem getting coal to keep them going. A good deal of 'borrowing' went on, and at night groups crept stealthily about the camp and always found a hoard somehow.

The morale of the camp was very high. Though the bulk of the men and women were British, many nationalities were represented. The Commonwealth Air Training Plan was in full swing, with increasing numbers of Australians, Canadians and New Zealanders figuring amongst the aircrew.

From all walks of life they came; some of the aircrew being pimply-faced youngsters barely out of school. Not many from the pre-war regular Air Force were to be seen, except perhaps among the ground staff. Many duties formerly handled by men were handed over to WAAFs and they did sterling work on such duties as driving tractors and crew trucks. The ground crews were, in the main, a little older than the aircrew; many were married with families and had been established in a wide variety of trades prior to hostilities. What a grand bunch they were too.

Each ground crew built themselves a hut on the edge of the dispersals. The crew which I joined had made a fine job from bits of Anderson shelter, timber and other oddments, and it was quite cosy inside. A neat garden had been laid out, though for much of the time it seemed to be a quagmire. Some crews went one better and erected rustic trelliswork, and even vegetables were planted.

We really loved our own allotted Lanc. She was fussed over like a new car, though we did not always get a brand new machine fresh from the factory. She was as much ours of course as the aircrew to whom she was assigned. She was swept and cleaned inside, and woe betide anyone who left a cigarette end around or was sick and said nothing.

Naturally, the enemy sometimes took a hand. If a kite came back from ops peppered with holes and jagged edges, we would jokingly curse the aircrew for not being more careful!

It was a proud boast to start the engines first time, regardless of the weather. However, a snag such as a sudden mag drop could not be helped. The Squadron Engineering Officer and the 'Chiefy' were always on hand to help sort out a ticklish problem. Tools were in short supply but we improvised and some ingenious concoctions resulted.

Patching and replacing parts would mean a long toil, and many were the times we worked day and night without a break, for it was a matter of pride to get one's kite back in the line as quickly as possible. The weather was perhaps our biggest enemy; soaked to the skin or blue with cold, we would be kept going with constant mugs of piping hot tea, brewed on our own stove. A wartime airfield was quite a pleasant place in summer, and on hot days we would strip down to the waist, even sunbathing when it was quiet.

In off-duty hours we made many friends with the local populace. Every evening the local pubs were packed, and the civilians were most tolerant of this huge invasion. Perhaps the favourite pub was *The White Hart* at Lissington, but with so many small villages near by, all the pubs were visited. Added to the RAF contingent were the Army, who had a camp near Wragby, and girls of the Land Army who were helping local farmers. All got on with one another surprisingly well, though a lot of friendly rivalry existed as to who could get all the girls!

Relations with the aircrews were excellent. During their tour of ops we got to know a crew very well. Often we would play cricket, football or have a round or two at cards over a brew-up at the hut when take-off was delayed. This was particularly so during the summer and autumn of 1944, when the second front opened and the daylight trips began in earnest.

In the dark grim days of 1943, with the Battle of the Ruhr in full swing, and again in the winter of 1943/4 – the Battle of Berlin – losses were heavy and few crews got past ten trips. Some were unlucky, going down on the last five. When a crew did not return there would be glum faces, but within a day or two a new crew would arrive and the whole cycle would begin again.

Once a kite was airborne we would take it in turns to wait up for her, and always there would be some of us to greet the crew when they returned. After each operation we would proudly paint on a bomb symbol with a stencil up on the kite's nose, and much friendly competition existed as to who had the kite with the most ops.

Some seemed to lead charmed lives, lasting for months on end, while others lasted but a week or two. From D-Day onwards, things became somewhat easier and kites began to tot up impressive totals. We heard a lot about veterans on other squadrons having reached a century, but the nearest we got was when 'Shiny Twelve' achieved it with their N-Nan. What a party followed!

While we would occasionally go out for a drink with a crew during their tour, there was always a free evening's beer when they finished their tour. Riotous parties at the 'Snake Pit' (officially known as the *Saracen's Head*) in Lincoln, or the *George* at Market Rasen would follow; then within a day or two they would be gone, usually being sent to an OTU or HCU as instructors. Once in a while one would lob in while on a cross-country exercise but, despite firm promises to keep in touch, one never did.

With the end of the war in Europe, the station took on a different atmosphere: gone was the old spirit. The whole camp was drastically run-down and most of us were posted. Now, 25 years on, memories of those stirring days have dimmed somewhat, but never will I forget. I would not have missed it for worlds.

CREW HUT *463 Squadron ground crew take a breather outside their gaudily-painted hut at Waddington. These huts, though crudely built, provided welcome shelter for both air and ground crews on bleak wind- and rain-swept airfields.*

Not all were of such sound construction. This one at Holme-on-Spalding Moor had been knocked together out of surplus Anderson shelter sections by 101 Squadron ground crew.

EASTER EGG *Ground crew of 424 'Tiger' Squadron RCAF send their own message to the enemy from Skipton-on-Swale, East Yorkshire. The raid was on Heide Oil Refinery, Hemming-stadt, March 20/21, 1945 and F/Lt J. F. Thomas, RCAF, and his crew having the honour of delivery (in BI, RF128 QB-V).*

BRIEFING

A HOLIDAY ABROAD *9 Squadron crews at Bardney in happy mood at briefing – in this case for Operation 'Bellicose', the first 'Shuttle Bombing' raid by Bomber Command.*

Bombing Freidrichshaven on June 20/21, 1943, 5 Group Lancs landed in North Africa and attacked Spezia on the return journey three nights later.

The hut is typical of the wartime approach to building, being completely utilitarian and functional.

Note the aircraft recognition models.

THE TENSION MOUNTS *As the large map at the end of the briefing room is uncovered revealing the target, the air is filled with deriding groans or lively chatter.*

The target is described and reason for attacking it, together with the latest gen on the weather and defences, followed by the tactics to be employed.

A 115 Squadron briefing at Witchford.

CREW CONFERENCE Sergeant Frank Collis of 207 Squadron checks over the final route and target details with his crew. In the foreground is the navigator's Dalton computer.

A normal Lancaster crew numbered seven – pilot, navigator, flight engineer, wireless operator (distinguished in this photo by the fist-and-sparks motif on his sleeve), bomb aimer/front gunner, mid-upper and rear gunners. Until 1943, there were isolated occasions when a crew member other than the pilot might be captain, but, subsequently, all pilots were captains, regardless of their rank.

The formation of early crews was a leftover from twin-engined bomber days and, until mid-1942, a Lancaster crew consisted of two pilots (the second doing the job later taken over by flight engineers), front gunner, observer, who navigated and dropped the bombs, first and second wireless operators, the latter being the mid-upper gunner (until mid-1942 all wireless operators were trained air gunners) and rear gunner.

In the early days of Lanc operations, with aircraft in short supply, some pilots did almost a complete tour as 'second dickey' until they were given their own Lanc and crew, when flight engineers became available. Later, a new squadron pilot would normally do his first op as flight engineer with an experienced crew.

Prelude to Hell

John Shelton

What was it like to go to war in the air? Which were the worst moments? The take-off? The outward journey? The bombing run? The ordeal of fighters, or flak?

Almost without exception those who flew bombers will tell you it was that last hour or so before the actual take-off. All along you secretly hoped for a cancellation, but the nearer loomed the time for take-off, the greater became the feeling of apprehension.

The tension really began to mount as you collected your gear, then caught the crew bus. By the time you reached your kite's dispersal, and had a last look round in the fading light, your nerves were becoming really stretched. As you climbed aboard and the door shut irrevocably behind you, the moment of truth arrived, the instant when stark reality replaced the sense of unreality which had prevailed all day since your name had appeared on the battle order.

You had really to force down the feeling of fear which now gripped you as you went through the checks, mouth dry, voice sounding an octave above normal. With engines running and take-off only moments away, the tension reached its peak. If you were going to abdicate, now was the time to do so. Once airborne and with work to do, it wasn't so bad, but oh, that last hour!

This feature, by John Shelton, describes vividly the sensations of those last minutes before a raid.

"Last night a strong force of Lancasters and Halifaxes of Bomber Command successfully attacked targets in the Ruhr. Extensive damage was done to marshalling yards and . . ."

A terse news bulletin . . . tired crews in restless sleep . . . the Merlins of dispersed Lancasters silent.

Some fourteen hours ago, the final briefings had been completed, the eggs and bacon had been downed to a backcloth of brittle cheerfulness and idle chatter. This, the prelude, was the worst of all. The whining Bedford truck arrives to transport crews to their aircraft, and all the necessary kit is carelessly slung aboard followed by a group of young, seemingly carefree men, hardly men at all and yet, because of their garb, appearing older than their years. They bear no resemblance to the young men in the streets outside; they are a race apart, a race belonging to aircraft, living in a world unreal to others. Bulbous flying jackets and boots disguise the frames within as the truck begins its jerky, unsprung journey towards the waiting aircraft at dispersal. Fresh cigarettes are lighted from the stub of a finished one as the truck heads for the expanse of tarmac and grass away from the cluster of camouflaged buildings, away from civilisation.

The airfield is quiet on this summer's evening, the sun spreading a mellow light, casting shadows many times longer than their owners. The Lincolnshire countryside personifies England, save for this plateau with its group of clinically stark buildings and hangars, and the runway running like a gigantic scar across its face. And standing at intervals around the plateau, these machines of war – the Lancasters of Bomber Command, these pregnant monsters that will give birth over the cities of Germany, in their drab coat of black stained with oil, threadbare in parts through erosion by the elements. Those two powerful looking legs supporting the aggressive body sniffing the air, its shoulders hunched, looking restless when tethered to Mother Earth, waiting for that truckload of unruly looking mortals who alone can cut its leash and allow it to soar into its natural element, where it will purr its contentment for hours on end.

Why is it the airfield always looks so much cleaner and less like an airfield in the late evening? It seems a good place to be, though not perched precariously on the side board of this infernal truck, but walking the WAAF from the ops room around its perimeter past the sleeping Lancasters, shrouded like falcons. You wish that were possible; that the truck and its noisy occupants could suddenly vaporise and leave you there alone. But its brakes suddenly project you forwards and then back and some wag shouts, "Terminus!" And you are over the side, tugging and pulling at your gear with its straps and leads and bags, and making your ungainly way to the open door. Around the aircraft are scattered those lucky dogs who will keep their feet on terra firma after you have gone, probably to walk that WAAF around to the NAAFI, the ground staff who, throughout the day, have watered and fed the beast, preparing it for its role in the ceaseless programme of destruction and fear.

Once inside you are aware of the smell peculiar to aircraft alone, a mixture of paint, dope, metal, oil – a smell that can play havoc with a delicate stomach even before take-off. There is general activity within; kit to be stowed; the pilot going through his now familiar checks and routines. The door finally closes, the ladder is stowed, and once more you are in this claustrophobic environment, the sun's rays shafting through the massive greenhouse above the pilot's cabin. You can hear the directions and instructions exchanged between the pilot and the ground crew far below, and then the first of those throbbing Merlins breaks into life, momentarily coughing and spluttering before settling into a rhythmic cycle. The instruments and radio sets vibrate slightly in their chipped, black crackle-finished mountings. One by one the four engines augment the

45

sound that vibrates every rivet. The wash from those massive props plays around the tailplane and makes the Lancaster dance lightly on its tailwheel, and the grass behind flattens itself against the soil.

Through the window can be seen other Lancasters along the line, coming into life, and there you stand as first one engine note rises and falls and then another. Eventually the power reaches an even sustained pitch and slowly the beast moves forward. There is a squeal of protest from the brakes as the pilot steers his mount on to the perimeter track. Again the brakes squeal, and the aircraft lurches forward and then relaxes. The long taxi to the end of the active runway. A long meandering line of Lancasters weighed down by their maximum burden, appearing as clumsy as plodding elephants around a circus ring.

The shaft of sunlight through the small window beside you sweeps slowly over the scuffed floor of the aircraft as it moves slowly round the perimeter track until those brakes squeal once more and you spin round and stop, lined up on the active runway, conscious of the wash from the preceding aircraft at full power for take-off. Finally the four Merlins raise their voices in full cry and for a moment the aircraft is checked in its urgency to take flight, and then the brakes are released and she surges forward, slowly at first, so slowly it seems, gradually gathering speed. Up front the pilot plays his throttles to check and compensate the torque produced by those lashing props. The runway flashes past the window, its rubber-scarred surface looking like some gigantic endless belt. The take-off run seems to go on and on as she rises on to the main wheels and the wings flex to lift the tremendous fuel and bombload. At long last the bumps suddenly diminish and fade away and she is airborne. The boundary fence and Chance light disappear behind you, and there is the flat Lincolnshire countryside, its predominant brownness scattered with shadows. The dusk is already beginning to appear to the east as the Lancaster reaches for altitude, on course for its rendezvous with the main flock. And now you are busy and because of this the tension eases somewhat. Yes, it's that prelude which is the worst of all – it always is.

INTENSE CONCENTRATION *as F/Lt G. Murtough, bombing leader of 463 Squadron RAAF, briefs his bomb aimers at Waddington for their vital part in the night's work which lies ahead, April 1944.*

OUT TO THE KITES

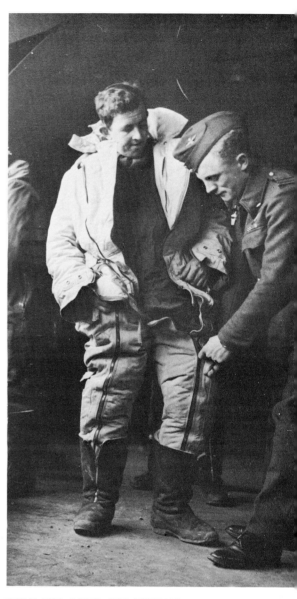

THE LOCKER ROOM *Briefing over, the crews collect their cumbersome gear, watched anxiously by one of the many WAAFs who tended their kit and packed their chutes. These 9 Squadron crews are bound for Stettin on the night of January 5/6, 1944.*

IT'LL BE COLD UP THERE
F/Sgt C. T. Akers, an Aussie, on his first tour, gets a helping hand with his unwieldy heated suit from his Gunnery Leader, F/Lt Bill Hill, on his third tour.

101 Squadron, Ludford Magna, before an attack on Berlin, January 20/21, 1944. The turrets were the coldest spots in a Lancaster, particularly the rear gunner's position where, with the centre panel removed, temperatures of minus 40°C could be experienced. Frostbite was a common occupational hazard.

The gunners' kapok suits were known as 'Taylor Suits', being bright yellow and having their own built-in Mae Wests.

THE LAST RITES *A last fag and forced joke by 101 Squadron air gunners at Ludford Magna before leaving for Berlin, January 20/21, 1944.*

NIGHT SCENE *A 44 Squadron BI, veteran of 72 ops, R5729 KM-A, at Dunholme Lodge, is caught by the lights of the crew bus as it drops the crew off at the 'terminus' before a raid on Berlin, January 2/3, 1944.*

Bomb doors would normally remain open until engines were started unless there had been a last-minute run-up to clear a minor snag, or unless the load was mines.

On this night, in the hands of P/O N. J. Lyford, RAAF, and crew, she was hit by flak and had to return on three engines. Perhaps it was an omen, because only a few nights later, with a different crew, she was lost without trace over Brunswick.

SOME WALK *Conditions on wartime airfields could be grim, particularly during bad weather. This is a typical scene at Ludford Magna, home of 101 Squadron, more often than not known as 'Mudford Magna'.*

SOME RIDE *A last minute check of gear by 9 Squadron crews as they assemble at the trucks which will take them to dispersal. The tension is reflected in the crews' faces before one of the devastating attacks on Hamburg in July 1943 (Operation Gomorrah).*

In the foreground are two yellow pigeon carriers. Each Lancaster would take two on operations in the early days but the practice was soon discontinued.

SOME PEDAL *This 106 Squadron crew cycles out to dispersal at Syerston, Notts., on a mild autumn evening in 1942.*

Squadron bikes were standard issue and, though each station would have several hundred, they were always in short supply.

The BI Lanc in the background is W4118 ZN-Y Admiral Prune, the mount of the Squadron CO, W/Cdr Guy Gibson, and shared with his 'B' Flight Commander S/Ldr 'Dim' Wooldridge.

THANKS FOR THE LIFT *On a cold, dark winter night in January 1944, F/O A. E. Manning and his 9 Squadron crew disembark at dispersal. This is their last chance for a cigarette and, although each man appears outwardly calm, inwardly the tension mounts and the stomachs tighten. Their destination, Stettin, one of the most heavily defended targets, deep in northeast Germany on the Polish border. Nine hours of hell ahead.*

THE WAITING GAME *Crews would often have to wait around at dispersal during the summer and autumn of 1944 in particular when, with the allied armies advancing on the Continent, targets were mostly tactical and could change rapidly.*

Sometimes there would be several briefings and false alarms in one day –

a great strain on the nerves. The time would be passed by playing cricket or football, a game of cards, or just lying on the grass and waiting for the 'off'.

At Witchford in June 1944 an all-NCO crew of 115 Squadron check the target details (left) and (below) enter their kite, KO-E.

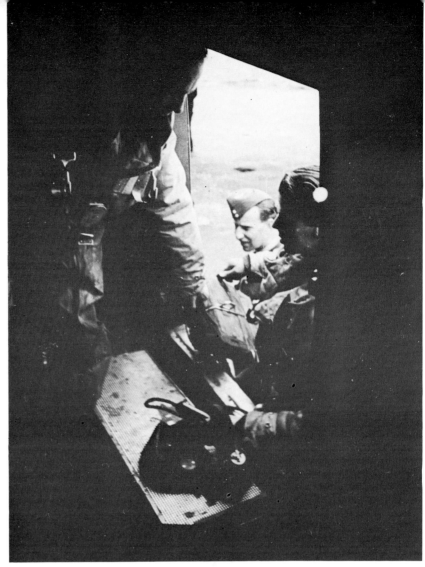

'A WELCOME CUPPA' *at the NAAFI van, always a comforting sight on a cold, blustery night, with take-off put back and crews kept hanging about at dispersal.*

Here W/Cdr Gomm and his 467 Squadron crew enjoy a hot brew at Bottesford in the winter of 1943. Of Brazilian descent, Gomm typifies the many nationalities flying with the RAF in the cause of freedom.

HERE WE GO AGAIN – ALL ABOARD *As the evening draws in, Sgt John McIntosh and his crew of 207 Squadron board their aircraft at Langar, May 1943. The series of photos which follow show the crew at their stations.*

INTERIORS

THE DREADED MAIN SPAR
*Once inside, the crew grope their way
along the dark narrow fuselage. Here
(above left) the wireless operator, Sgt
John Hyde, negotiates the main spar,
with which many a shin lost an argument.*

'NAV' IN HIS OFFICE *The navigator, Sgt Iain H. Nicholson, dons his
helmet (left). After take off, few navs
would venture outside their curtained-off
compartment.*

RADIO CHECK *The wireless op
checks his set (above). His position was
the warmest in the kite, right beside the
warm air outlet, and he would often be
sweating when the others were shivering.*

BLIND BOMBING AID *The H2S
set (below). The scanner was housed in
a ventral radome and the trace threw a
negative-style picture of the ground
below on the screen. It is rumoured that
it acquired its name while in the early
experimental stage. A particularly
high-ranking officer was somewhat
suspicious of the scientists' claims and is
reputed to have said, 'It smells – call it
H2S'.*

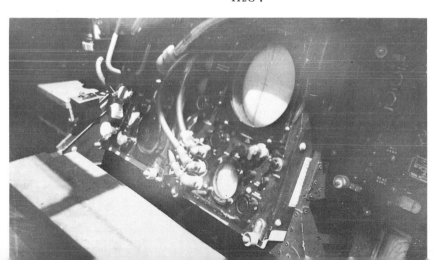

EQUIPMENT CHECK *The Lancaster gave the bomb aimer the best view of any wartime bomber, particularly when the larger blister was fitted from 1943 onwards. Later in the war, a downward and rearward-sighting blister was added just below the nose. Equipment had to be thoroughly checked before take-off. Sgt Desmond Ball checks his panel (above) and front guns (below).*

For take-off and landing the bomb aimer was not supposed to stay in the nose, but many did. With parachute harness on, it was no easy job to squeeze under the flight engineer's seat to return to the front compartment.

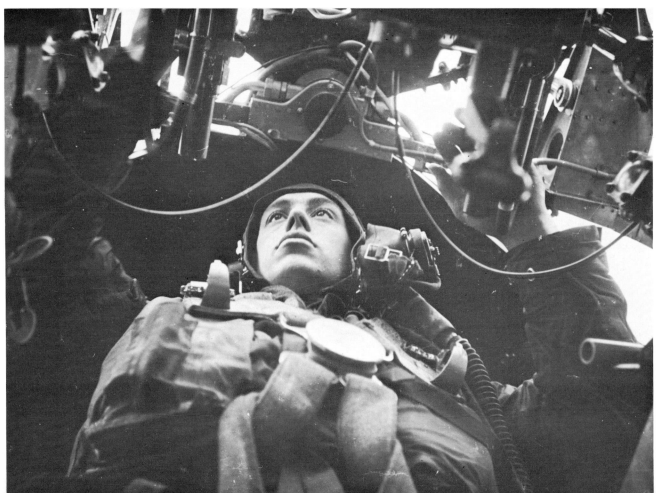

BOX OF TRICKS *The bomb aimer's panel. Top left are the 16 bomb selector switches. Below them is the timing device for stick-bombing, the dial bottom-right being for selection of the timing interval between bombs. To the right, in the centre of the panel, is the selector box for order of dropping, it being essential to keep the aircraft balanced by correct spread of bomb-release from the 33-foot long bomb bay. Master switch and camera controls are centre top, and photo-flare releases are on the small separate panel below. Extreme top right is the 4,000lb bomb slip heater which prevented a hang-up through freezing. The bomb-release button can be seen in its stowed position, with a small guard above it to prevent accidental depressions of the 'tit'.*

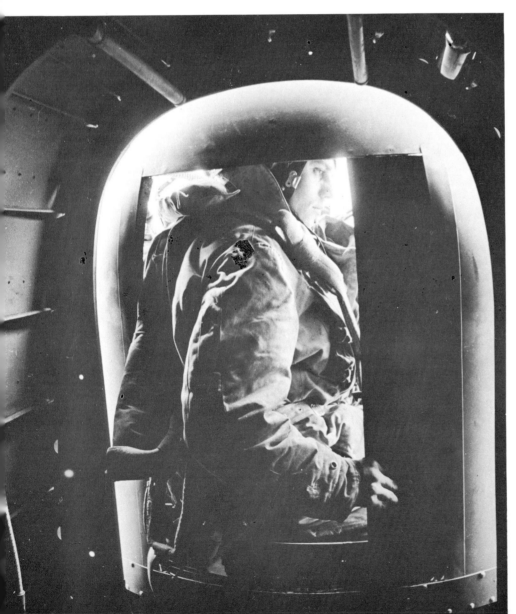

THE LONELIEST PLACE *The rear gunner, Sgt Roland Middleton, closes the doors of his turret. His was a most unenviable spot – cut off from the others except by intercom. Quite the loneliest position in the kite.*

TAIL-END CHARLIES *Three stages in rear turret development. (Right) the original turret of 1942 vintage. Gunners had difficulty seeing through the centre perspex panel which often became scratched, misted or frosted up and it was removed as shown (below left) on a 186 Squadron BI, NG149 XY-G) at Stradishall, January 1945. The gunner is Sgt Jack Collins, hence the title 'Jack's Joint'.*

Though Frazer Nash turrets were standard in nose, mid-upper and tail, a new turret appeared in 1944, made by Rose Bros. It was equipped with two .5in Brownings and was large enough to house two gunners. 1 Group were the main users.

Sgt Ted Eyles of 101 Squadron in a Rose tail turret (below right) early in 1945. Under the turret is the 'Monica' radar aerial operated by the wireless operator to detect enemy fighters.

MID-UPPER *The mid-upper gunner had the best all round view. Getting into the restricted space of the turret was a difficult task; getting out in a hurry when the aircraft was in trouble could be even more difficult. It was also a highly vulnerable spot with little or no armour protection, and the roundels below were an ideal aiming point for enemy fighters from any angle.*

COCKPIT *Clean and functional – the 'office' with the pilot's position on the left and flight engineer on the right. Not an inch of space was wasted. For training, extension arms for a second control wheel and rudders could be fitted, but very few operational Lancasters were fitted for two-pilot operation.*

DUSK RUN UP 1 *With chocks still firmly in position, the Hercules engines of this MkII of 426 'Thunderbird' Squadron RCAF are 'given the gun' by the pilot until the props are almost invisible at full revs against the setting sun. Checking –*
Pressures & temperatures – All OK. *Hydraulics* – Flaps down, up and indicating. *Bomb doors* – Closed. *Booster pumps* – Off. *Rad. Shutters* – Open. *Magnetos* – Checked and serviceable.

DUSK RUN UP 2 *In the gathering dusk, anxiously watched by three ground crew, Sgt McIntosh finishes the engine checks on BIII* ED802, EM-M, *in her Langar dispersal before calling the pre-taxi checks –*
Ground/Flight switch – On flight. *Nav. lights* – On. *Altimeter* – QFE is set. *Instruments* – All serviceable. *Suction* – 4½. *Rad. Shutters* – Open. *Brakes* – Pressures OK.

First flight on ops

Lance Connery

Ask anyone who served in aircrew in the 1939–45 fracas if he remembers his first bomber operation. He will.

It's the kind of high adventure one never forgets. Even the small details stay fresh in the mind long after most other operational flights have slipped away into memory's limbo.

There's good reason for that sense of vivid recollection. The first op is a long-awaited consummation of hundreds of hours of flying training between seven young men. Up to that point nothing that has gone before seems really consequential. For many new crews, the first trip spells the ultimate difference between success and failure, life and death.

It was no secret during the war that aircrew losses on the first five operations were heavy. Bomber Command came to expect an average loss of four per cent on each trip, though individual operations sometimes cost as high as ten per cent in aircraft missing. For brand new crews the average was much higher; it was the old hands who made a habit of coming back.

At one time it was squadron custom to send a crew on leave after the first operational flight. The trouble was that when they returned to make a second trip they were apt to go missing, either from over-confidence, or because they were not perfectly fit (celebrating can be overdone!).

In my own group the rule was changed to, "No leave until five successful operations are completed." The practice cut the ratio of crew losses appreciably.

World War II may have been the last conflict in which bomber crews will operate in that fashion. The days of heavy bombers are going fast, and the guided missile promises to replace even the pilot, who may eventually become a highly-trained ground technician, rather than the airborne master of a high-flying apparatus of mass destruction.

I well remember my own first trip. It was the night of March 24, 1944, at a Lancaster station called Bardney, near the centuries-old city of Lincoln. The squadron was one of the oldest in the RAF. Its motto was, 'Throughout the night we fly', but everyone used the unofficial motto of, 'There's always bloody something', which dated back to the squadron's Wimpeys in the pioneering days of 1941.

The station wasn't a glamorous establishment like those permanent RAF bases with cut-stone manor houses for billets and messing. It was a sprawling layout of Nissen huts with a few larger buildings of the same ugly but highly functional construction. Two thousand souls called it home. Two miles away was the village of Bardney, which had only one thousand population and no fewer than seven pubs!

That day the squadron buzzed with pre-ops gossip.

Since the petrol load was a relatively large one, we knew it was going to be a long trip, but hadn't the least idea where. Not till briefing-time did we know, and the news was not conducive to morale for a sprog crew. The target was to be Berlin. Now Berlin had already been subjected to mass attacks by the RAF fifteen times, and this, though we didn't know it till later, was to be the sixteenth and last such large-scale sortie against the German capital.

There were about 900 heavy bombers ordered to fly that night, in two-minute waves of 180 aircraft each, scheduled to reach the target at various heights between 19,000 and 23,000 feet. Timing was of the utmost importance, not only to reduce the chances of collision over the target, but to swamp the defences by as concentrated an attack as possible.

After briefing we adjourned for the night flying meal, in which the squadron's happy practice was to include a precious fried egg. Other squadrons were inclined to serve the egg with the post-operational meal, but our people argued it wasn't fair, since missing crews hadn't had their eggs! That may have been consoling to some; to us it sounded positively sinister.

We took off at 19.00 hrs, climbing slowly to height in our heavily-laden Lancaster, then followed the track to the specified turning points. As we neared the target the Lancaster started to heave and pitch in the slip-stream of other aircraft, and an unholy mess of flak came up from the city. Small bits clattered against our aircraft, but our bomb aimer got the load away successfully and we headed for home.

There were fighters in the offing, so we jinked about a bit in the usual evasive action, and finally settled down to the long trip back. There was low cloud over Bardney, so we were diverted to Little Snoring (those wonderful English place-names!) and flew from there to base later in the day. Seven hours and thirty-five minutes was the duration of the operation.

We'd been pretty lucky. There were 17 small holes in the aircraft, none of them bigger than an inch in diameter, and all in non-vital places. Lancasters were wonderful operational bombers; they would fly well on three engines, not badly on two, and they could land on one.

Not all first trips were so uneventful. Another crew had no fewer than seven combats with fighters on their first operation and happily came home unharmed, though with a few chunks of aircraft missing.

After Berlin, the rest was anti-climax and we had no tougher target in the tour. It's hard to recall the rest of them. There's nothing like the first.

TAXYING AND MARSHALLING

QUEUE HERE FOR KASTROP
On some occasions the fully-laden aircraft would be taxied round the peritrack to a convenient holding point and shut down until it was time to go. These Lancasters of 428 'Ghost' Squadron RCAF stand tightly packed near the runway's end at Middleton St George, all ready to go when the time comes. A gunner and two ground crew take advantage of the pause to do some last-minute tinkering. In an hour the whole area will shake as a hundred Merlins are started up. If a Lanc went u/s at this stage, it could cause chaos, and towing vehicles were always on hand to haul them clear if necessary.

The night's raid was to be on the synthetic oil plant at Kastrop-Rauxel, November 21/22, 1944, a night on which Bomber Command put up 1,100 aircraft and attacked five separate targets. The following figures may help to illustrate the magnitude of the task involved in preparing for an operation by a thousand bombers: over 2,000,000 gallons of petrol, 70,000 gallons of oil, and 5,000 gallons of coolant go into the aircraft themselves. Over 4,500 tons of bombs may be required, plus 10,000,000 rounds of ammunition for the guns. Thirty thousand bicycles, 3,500 bomb trolleys, and 6,000 other vehicles are employed. Fifteen million litres of oxygen, 8,000 pints of coffee and 6,000lb of food also go into the aircraft.

STAND BY TO TAXI *The signal given, a Lanc moves out of dispersal to queue up on the perimeter track at the end of the runway.*

Turning was achieved by giving the outer engine a burst and straightening up by using the opposite outer, keeping a hand on the brake lever to stop her running away.

This is the time of day to which the Lancaster seemed to belong – the fading light; the setting sun highlighting spinners, turrets and cockpit.

GENTLY DOES IT *Taxying a fully-laden Lancaster along the winding narrow peri-track could be a tricky business.* KB839 *VR-D,* Daisy, *a Canadian-built BX of 419 "Moose" Squadron RCAF, is eased gently along at Middleton St George prior to a daylight op in 1945.*

In the background can be seen a ground crew's hut, complete with the Squadron insignia.

M – MOTHER, CLEAR TO LINE UP *The Chance light guides the way as* BIII ED724, *PM-M of 103 Squadron, nears the end of the runway on a dark night at Elsham Wolds, early in March 1943.*

Paraffin-filled 'goosenecks' line the runway while a canopy of searchlights pierce the sky to show the cloudbase.

Often all the airfield lights would suddenly go out – intruders were about!

WAITING THEIR TURN *Who said the kiwi has no wings? Lancs from the No. 75 New Zealand Squadron queue up for take-off at Mepal in March 1945. (Nearest is* BI, PB820 *JN-V, F/Lt D. Clements, RNZAF, and crew.)*

By April 1945, Bomber Command could put up over 1,000 Lancs alone and an Order of Battle drawn up on the 19th shows 52 squadrons so equipped, comprising a total strength of 1,375 machines.

TAKE-OFF

G – GEORGE – READY FOR TAKE-OFF *A spare 'trolley acc' and standby ground crew are on hand in case a kite stalls and blocks the runway. Final pre-take-off checks are made: Autopilot – Clutch in, cock out. D.R. Compass – Set and operating. Pitot heater – On. Trimmer – Elevator two forward, others to neutral. Pitch – Fully fine. Fuel – Contents checked, Master cocks on, No. 2 tanks selected,* Crossfeeds off, Booster pumps on. *Superchargers – M Gear. Air Intake – Cold. Rad. Shutters – Auto. Flaps – Set to take off and indicating.*

A green from the caravan will send 'George', BIII DV236, of 101 Squadron on its way to Berlin January 20/21, 1944, from Ludford Magna, piloted by Sgt Sandy Sandford. The FIDO pipes, looking surprisingly frail, border the runway.

ABOUT TO LIFT OFF *Right hand on the throttles, thumb advancing the port outer to stop her swinging, stick forward to get the tail up, deft use of the rudders to keep her straight, the needle creeps up to the 90 knots mark and the 'point of no return'. In the hands of 'A' Flight Commander, S/Ldr Tom Rippingale, A-Able NX573, P4-A, a brand new 153 Squadron kite, is about to become 'unstuck' at Scampton in 1945. Keen eyes will note the dorsal turret forward of the standard position, this being one of 50 BI (BVII interim) Lancs produced by Austin Motors pending the introduction of the BVII with a Martin turret.*

GOOD LUCK *There was always a gathering of station personnel to wave off each kite regardless of the weather. This is a scene (above) at Elsham Wolds on July 4, 1944, as BI* LM227 *I-Item of 576 Squadron begins to roll at the end of the runway on the first of the 100 operations she was to complete by the cessation of the war in Europe.*

Pilotless bomber

Jimmy Griffiths

When something went wrong on take-off it could mean disaster for an aircraft heavily laden with high-explosive and incendiary bombs.

In April 1944, P/O Jimmy Griffiths and his crew arrived at Elsham Wolds to join 576 Squadron as 'new boys'. To their dismay, they were allocated the oldest Lancaster on the station.

One week and three operations later, their Flight Commander, whose posting to PFF had just come through, yielded to their protests and let them have his new Lanc BIII, LM527 UL-U². It was a decision which very nearly cost the crew their lives.

Following the abortive take-off described below, the young Scots skipper and his crew reverted to their original BIII, ED888 UL-M², in which they went on to complete their tour. Indeed, this veteran Lanc was later to become Bomber Command's top-scoring 'heavy', with 140 operational sorties to its credit.

Briefing was over, final checks had been made on the aircraft and the crews were relaxing in the few minutes left before take-off time, on a lovely spring evening, April 30, 1944 – target Maintenon.

I was thrilled at the prospect of flying one of the latest Lancasters, so much superior to old M², the veteran aircraft I had flown on my first three operations.

The runway in use was the shortest one on the 'drome and necessitated revving up against the brakes, almost to full power, before take-off, similar to the method employed on aircraft carriers.

Time to go – always a tense moment – and we are soon lined up on the runway making the last quick cockpit check. "Rich mixture", "Propellers in fine pitch", "Flaps up", "Fuel gauges OK". Ready to go! Throttles are opened slowly against the brakes until the aircraft throbs with power, straining and vibrating until the brakes can barely hold her. Brakes are released and we leap forward. Keep straight by use of throttles and rudder and ease the control column forward to bring the tail up. "Full power!" the engineer takes over the throttles and opens them fully, locking them in that position. The tail is now off the ground, giving full control on the rudders for keeping straight, and the airspeed indicator is creeping slowly up towards the take-off speed.

Something's wrong! We are nearing the end of the runway and haven't yet reached take-off speed. We should be airborne by now! A glance at the instruments shows that, whilst all four engines are running smoothly, they are not giving maximum power. Too late to stop –

the fence at the end of the runway is right under our nose – speed is dangerously low.

I yank back on the stick and the aircraft labours painfully off the ground. We are on the point of stalling and I have to level out, praying that I'll miss the small hill beyond the fence. I have just time to shout "Wheels up!" when – *Crash!!!*

The aircraft shudders violently; the nose kicks up at a dangerous angle and I instinctively push the stick forward to avoid stalling. I ease the stick back quickly, flying a matter of inches above the ground which, providentially, is sloping downwards. I nurse the aircraft along, still hugging the grass. The speed slowly increases beyond the danger mark and very gradually the altimeter needle creeps away from ZERO in answer to a slight backward pressure on the stick.

I start to breathe again, brushing the perspiration from my brow and feel a cold chill up my spine as I think of the load of high explosive bombs beneath my feet hanging on their inadequate-looking hooks. "A fine start to an operation," I was thinking; but more was to follow.

We were climbing very slowly and I realised from the sluggishness of the controls that all was not well. Charlie Bint, the bomb aimer, climbed down into his compartment in the nose and was able to inform me that the starboard wheel had not fully retracted! It must have taken the full force of the impact into the hill. No amount of pumping on the emergency hydraulic hand pump would budge it either up or down, and I knew that we would be unable to continue on the mission as it was taking too much power and consequently too much fuel to overcome the drag of the damaged wheel.

I flew east, still climbing very slowly, meaning to jettison the bombload in the North Sea and return to make an emergency landing.

One hour after take-off we had reached 9,000 feet and were circling a few miles east of Grimsby, the North Sea looking cold and deserted underneath. I depressed the lever which should have opened the bomb doors but no red warning light appeared! This was serious. I dived steeply and pulled out quickly in the hope of shaking the doors open, but to no avail. The flight engineer reported that the tank for the hydraulic fluid was completely dry. It was obvious that in our attempts to retract the damaged wheel we had pumped all the fluid into the atmosphere through a broken pipeline.

There was no alternative but to return to base for instructions. It was safe to break radio silence now that the rest of the squadron had been on their way for almost two hours. The WAAF radio telephonist lost no time in passing my message to the Flying Control Officer and very soon I was talking to the Station Engineering Officer and finally to the 'old man' himself.

We were ordered to make further experiments, but when we had tried everything it was finally apparent that we were saddled with a bomber fully laden with bombs which couldn't be released and a damaged undercarriage which would make landing a hazardous affair not to be contemplated when our bombload was enough to blow an aerodrome to pieces!

"Stand by," I was ordered and we circled round, wondering how long it would take them to reach a decision. Tommy Atherton, the navigator, brought me a cup of coffee out of his Thermos flask and we had a quiet crew conference. "What do you think they'll decide, Skip?" – this from Taffy, one of the gunners.

I spoke the thought that had been in my mind since the bomb doors had refused to budge. "How would you like to join the Caterpillar Club?" (This is a Club consisting of airmen who have baled out to save their lives.) There was a bit of joking, but it sounded rather forced and I called up the 'drome to ask them to speed up their decision.

"Reduce height to 5,000 feet and stand by!" I knew then that I had correctly assumed what the order would be – we were coming down to a level where a parachute wouldn't drift too far from the 'drome!

I reported again at 5,000 feet and the next instruction produced a stir of activity. "Fly upwind and order crew to bale out one at a time. Remain at controls and stand by." The crew needed no second bidding. Through they filed – two gunners, wireless operator, navigator and engineer, filling the confined space of the cockpit, their parachutes fixed firmly across their chests. Charlie was already in his compartment in the nose, opening the escape hatch in the floor. As they stepped quietly out of my sight to take their turn at jumping, each one shook my hand vigorously as he passed.

In a very short time I was left alone, and very much alone I felt. The roar of the engines seemed to grow louder, the controls seemed heavier and the aircraft seemed suddenly to be larger, more powerful, more sinister. "All out," I advised control.

"Circle and stand by," I was ordered. Then followed the loneliest few minutes of my life and I was glad to hear 'the voice' again. "Fly across the 'drome on an exact course of 080 degrees. Engage automatic pilot ('George'). When exact height and course being maintained – bale out!"

I welcomed the opportunity of having something to occupy my attention and spent quite a long time adjusting the controls until the aircraft was flying 'hands off' at exactly 5,000 feet on an exact course of 080 degrees.

I engaged the automatic pilot, made a few final adjustments and then, as the 'drome appeared ahead, I hurried down into the bomb aimer's compartment where the escape hatch lay open, almost invitingly.

I was glad that I had taken the precaution of having my parachute hooked on before the crew had gone and, with a final quick check, I crouched beside the hatch, my hand already clutching the steel handle of the ripcord. I sat on the edge of the hole and let my legs dangle. The rush of air immediately forced them against the underside of the aircraft and I allowed myself to roll out into space, head first.

I did four complete somersaults, seeing the four exhaust pipes of the aircraft glowing each time I turned over. I was counting one, two, three, four at each somersault and suddenly thought that I must be near the ground. I pulled the ripcord handle and it came away so easily that I remember gazing at my hand, which was still holding the handle, and thinking, "It hasn't worked!" Before I could feel any panic there was a rush of silk past my face, followed by a not too violent jerk and I found myself dangling comfortably under the silken canopy.

I felt a surge of absolute exhilaration and was grinning like a fool. I wish I could describe the feeling of power, of remoteness, of unreality, of sheer exuberance I felt. No wonder our paratroops are such grand fighters!

There was no rush of air to indicate downward speed and it came as quite a shock, on looking down, to see a field rushing up to meet me out of the darkness and a few scattered houses taking shape around it. I had hardly time to brace myself when I hit the ground, heels first, travelling backwards. I sat down with a bump, rolled over in a backward somersault and pressed the release catch to prevent being hauled along the ground. There was no need: the parachute flopped lazily over me and I lay still for a few moments, not believing that this was reality.

I bundled the parachute under my arm and trudged across the field in unwieldy flying boots towards a large house about fifty yards distant. Fortunately there was a telephone in the house and the old couple, whom I eventually wakened, plied me with questions and cups of tea until the car arrived from the 'drome.

All the crew had reported safe landings and some had already been picked up by the time I returned. There were many theories put forward regarding the part failure of the engines and it was finally decided that they must have been running on 'hot' air, a device used under icing conditions, which reduces the amount of power to each engine.

All this time the aircraft was flying steadily onwards towards enemy territory and we learned later that the Observer Corps had plotted its journey more than halfway across the North Sea, maintaining the height and course I had set.

The Duty Navigator who had given me the course computed that the fuel supply would last until the aircraft was somewhere in the Hamburg area. We can only guess the outcome.

Before abandoning the aircraft I had switched on every available light, and I often wonder what the Luftwaffe and the German AA gunners must have thought when they saw a large bomber approaching from the direction of England, lit up like a Christmas tree, flying steadily on a fixed course and blithely ignoring flak, searchlights and fighter attacks.

I like to think that 'George', guided by his saintly namesake, would point the aircraft in its final dive towards some important military objective, the destruction of which may have contributed in some way to the dramatic collapse of the Reich war machine which was soon to follow.

ALMOST AIRBORNE *The end of the runway looms closer as this heavily-laden Lanc of 419 'Moose' Squadron RCAF pounds along at Middleton St George early in 1944, with 3,000 rpm and +9 inches of boost on the clock. The pilot is already applying coarse right rudder to counteract the swing to port.*

AIRBORNE BY NIGHT *In the gathering darkness, a 467 Squadron RAAF Lanc (above right) thunders away from Waddington as the tower gives a green to the next one already lined up for take-off, for a raid on Bourg-Leopold May 11/12, 1944.*
"Brakes on – Brakes off; Undercarriage up; 2,850 rpm and plus 6."

AIRBORNE BY DAY *"Undercarriage up" and the wheels are already tucking backwards as this 218 'Gold Coast' Squadron Lanc (right) climbs out of Chedburgh for a daylight op on Oberhausen in December 1944 skippered by F/Lt "Wag" Walker. A loss of an engine at this, a critical point of take-off in a heavily-laden kite, could spell disaster.*

BLOW UP In a mighty mushroom of smoke and debris, a 4,000-pounder goes up at Croft on March 22, 1945, taking a Canadian-built Lanc X, KB832 WL-F of 434 'Bluenose' Squadron with it. Caught by an extraordinarily fierce gust of wind on take-off, the Lanc was lifted sideways and dumped on the right-hand side of the runway, coming to rest, minus undercarriage, in a cloud of earth and flame. F/O Horace Payne, RCAF, and crew escaped unhurt, but the bombload soon began to simmer as the 1,500 4lb incendiaries caught fire. 37 minutes later, at 11.27 hrs, the 'cookie' went off. Eight of 434's Lancasters had already taken off, but this crash prevented the rest of the Squadron from getting airborne for the raid on Hildesheim.

CLIMB OUT With: "Undercarriage up, lights out; Safety speed; Flaps up; 2,650 and plus four"; the pilot eases into a climbing turn to port to clear the airfield.

TIME TO SET COURSE SKIPPER – ZERO NINER ZERO MAGNETIC *In the last moments of daylight, a Lanc turns away to set course for enemy territory. Before doing so, it may have circled as far inland as the West Midlands to gain height and to wait for the rest of the main stream to join up. The sky would be full of heavily-laden aircraft, climbing and circling for perhaps an hour, straining upwards. Then at the set moment, all would turn eastwards, the Merlins would fade, and the sky would be suddenly empty and strangely silent.*

Once airborne, you would be on your own in the dark. Seldom would you see another aircraft save over the target and then perhaps just a fleeting glimpse of some poor chaps caught in a cone of searchlights and being peppered by flak; or a fiery red glow as a night fighter claims another victim.

EN ROUTE – HIGH LEVEL *No words can adequately describe this scene as a MkII wends its way towards the North Sea. What lies in store for the crew beyond the mountainous cloudscape?*

BOMBER COUNTRY *A 'G-H' radar-equipped 'vic' leader (distinguished by two yellow bars on the fins) from 149 'East India' Squadron, Methwold, just airborne over typical East Anglian countryside, spring 1945, waiting for the remainder of the vic to form up before setting course.*

149, like most 3 Group Lanc Squadrons, consisted of three flights, and this example, a BI, HK793, is from 'C' Flight.

Aft of the enlarged bomb bay is a hatch for a .303in machine gun (some kites had .5in) and many 3 Group Lancs not fitted with H2S had such a feature. The extra gunner was more often than not a 'spare bod' some of whom were Leading Aircraftsmen, even though the lowest rank of aircrew was officially Sergeant.

PLOUGHING A FURROW *This Lanc soon hit trouble. On take-off from Balderton for a raid on Politz, February 8, 1945, BI, PD348 9J-B, lost an engine just as she left the runway. Staggering along, fully laden, at dangerously low level, only a knot or two above stalling speed, F/O George Edge and his 227 Squadron crew were unable to turn back or gain height. Not daring to jettison the bombs for fear of blowing themselves out of the sky with their own 'cookie', they somehow nursed the kite along until a crash landing became inevitable. She was successfully pancaked in a cabbage field at Heath House Farm, near Bircham Newton in Norfolk. Miraculously, the bombs did not go off. Not surprisingly, the crew were in an extremely shocked state and when reached by the rescue party were discovered playing an imaginary game of cricket beside their crashed Lanc, quite oblivious to the seven tons of high explosives simmering nearby.*

OUTWARD BOUND *Climbing steadily away from the coast, this 619 Squadron Lanc heads eastwards, leaving the rear gunner to ponder on the view of Skegness pier below. Will he ever see it again?*

Once out to sea the guns will be tested. The 'can' has already been passed round – just as well to be comfortable.

Late guests

Edward Cook

In the spring of 1945, the allied armies were closing for the kill, and Hitler's vaunted Third Reich was crumbling fast.

Those aircrew unlucky enough to be shot down and to fall into civilian or police hands could expect little mercy. The German propaganda ministry had been working overtime inflaming the people against the 'Terror Fliers' and to be caught could mean a beating, stoning or even a lynching.

Those captured by the Wehrmacht often had to join in the retreat, suffering constant strafing by marauding allied fighters. For them it meant a succession of jails, barns or compounds. Many of the PoW camps were being abandoned and the inmates force-marched deep into the Fatherland.

At Mildenhall on Sunday, April 22, 1945, F/Lt Edward Cook and crew were to lead a 3 Group attack on Bremen. The British Second Army were within a few miles of the port, so little trouble was expected. The war seemed almost over. In fact, as they took off for the evening attack – their 28th operation – in Lanc BI, HK770 GI-T, they wondered if the war would end before they could complete their tour. Little did they realise what adventures lay ahead.

The following account is by the skipper, but each of his crew had similar lively experiences.

I was leading the 3 Group attack. At this stage of the war the Germans had become very cunning with their flak. They would throw up a green marker, and visually measure the distance between its bursting point and the leading aircraft. This usually happened in the last three minutes of the GH bombing run, and with minor adjustments they had a bead on the leading aircraft. As the whole principle of the GH radar demanded extremely accurate flying, evasive tactics were out of the question at this point. At 18.28 on that Sunday evening, two minutes short of the target, at 19,500 feet, there was a direct hit on my port outer engine. Fortunately, it hit on the outside of the nacelle away from the fuselage, and blew the engine out of the wing. It also took about six feet off the wing tip. The aircraft went into a steep diving turn to port, with fire in the wreckage where the engine had been. Normal fire drill accomplished nothing, and with the aircraft out of control, things began to look serious. I gave the order to jettison bombload at 18,000, and fortunately the bomb bay was open. With bombs gone, conditions did not improve and at 12,000 I made the decision to bale out the crew.

As my navigator, Mel Parry, went past to exit from the nose hatch, I pointed out to him that he would likely be a little late for church as it was already past 18.30. 'Mac' MacLaren, my flight engineer, inadvertently grabbed his chest-pack parachute by the ripcord instead of the lifting handle, and the only advice I could give him was to go out backwards through the nose hatch and hold as much of the parachute as he could until he was clear of the aircraft. This was apparently successful.

When everyone had gone, I made my first attempt to get out myself, and found it impossible. The moment I let the controls go to get out of the seat, the aircraft went into a screaming dive and started to roll. One good thing that this did was to put out the fire, and I decided that the only thing to do was to crash-land. I was very busy during the next couple of minutes, but fortunately, by a judicious mixing of trimtabs and controls, found that I was able to fly more or less in a straight line, admittedly with left wing low, but maintaining height at approximately 5,000 feet. With fingers crossed, I set course to the west.

I could hold the aircraft fairly steady between 105 and 110 knots without too much vibration. The course I set was as close as possible about 260 degrees true because I remembered that the surface wind was about 340 degrees true. There were heavy clouds to the south and I did not want to steer 270 degrees because of the long sea crossing. I thought the course I was steering would just about clear the Dutch Salient. I had no maps, and it was very annoying to see them floating past me and out of the front hatch, with all sorts of other papers. I had to steer a zigzag course through the cloud lanes and of course it was impossible to leave the controls to fire the Very pistol or switch on the IFF. I called 'Mayday' every three minutes on both UHF and VHF without reply for about 45 minutes before throwing my helmet away.

The clouds ahead thickened up without any lane, and the base looked to be about 2,000 feet. The port inner engine started to splutter; number 2 tank registered empty; number 1 registered about 30 gallons. I hit the balance cock but decided to come below the cloud base. It was now 20.45 hrs. The port inner engine was losing power rapidly. I was using full right rudder to keep straight, but still thought I might make England, as I was maintaining height. I suddenly sighted a forest out to starboard and thought I recognised Appeldoorn, so eased to the south, but 20 millimetre tracers scored hits on the rear of the fuselage. I was in Indian territory! I was soon out of range but three minutes later the 20 millimetres opened up again ahead of me. A Lancaster at 1,800 feet is, of course a sitting duck. I

74

was hit repeatedly and suddenly the starboard outer engine choked. As I got out of the seat the altimeter registered 1,200 feet, and although I went headfirst from the pilot's deck through the escape hatch in the nose, I doubt if my parachute started to open at more than 800 feet.

The aircraft crashed, exploded and burst into flames just before I came down, about two miles ahead of me, at 20.50 hrs. There were two explosions, and I later learned from the Germans that at least one and probably two of my 500lb bombs must have hung up; so it was just as well I never made that belly landing.

I was loose in the dykes for some little time, but unfortunately nightfall came just a shade too late, and I was caught in enfilading fire from each end of a dyke where I had arrived by a zigzag process.

The nearest village of any size to my point of entry into Holland is a place called Culemborg which is about 15 miles north-west of Tiel on the river Wall. The flak batteries which brought me down were at a place called Rijswijk. My plane came down a little south of the mid-point of a line between Maurik and Rijswijk. In 1959 I went back to the area, visited the farm and stood on the spot where the three Merlin engines are still buried, having sunk into the marsh when the Germans blew the dykes in late April. The ancient furrows, three of of them, are still visible, although there is no sign of the cow which I understand was blown to pieces by the exploding bombs. Parts of HK770 may easily be recognised holding up fences in the vicinity.

I touched down about 20.50 hrs on the south-west side of the Amsterdam Bovenrijn Canal, 90 degrees from Zoelmond about 4 kilometres, 330 degrees from Tiel about 8 kilometres, or 100 degrees from Culemborg 11 kilometres. The aircraft came down across the Canal, 075 degrees from my landing point, about 3 kilometres. I was picked up about 21.05 or 21.10 hrs by the Wehrmacht and taken about 6 kilometres west, to a farm at the other side of Zoelmond. There I slept the night in a barn with six German soldiers, had some black bread and cheese for breakfast, and was taken about 10.00 to the Divisional Headquarters of the Wehrmacht which was about two kilometres farther west. I had lunch with a Lieutenant-Colonel and a Major, was taken back to the village, and then, with two guards on bicycles, walked about 10 kilometres in a northwesterly direction, through Culemborg, and across the river, which I think is called the Neder Rijn, by cantilevered bridge.

Walking in flying boots was not exactly my idea of fun, so I took a stand and refused to walk any farther. The guards were rather nonplussed, but finally stopped a farm wagon and I rode in great style for about another nine kilometres to a small town. There I was introduced to a rather nasty SS man and had a little trouble. How-ever, I maintained my position and refused to walk, and finally, to·my great surprise and joy, a captured American jeep was provided to take me to Utrecht. Within another hour I was in the Utrecht jail, and by this time it was 21.00 hrs.

Since lunch time I had been carefully carrying one-quarter of a loaf of black bread, half an ounce of butter and one piece of cheese. From here on I should point out that the daily rations which were handed out, no matter where we were, at 12 noon, were one bowl (a little larger than a cup) of hot water which was called soup, two slices of black bread, two cubic inches of cheese and one cubic inch of meat (I think it was horse meat). Sundays were always feast days when the soup had meat in it.

So I arrived in Utrecht on the night of Monday April 23. There were two American pilots in the jail with me and on the 26th we were moved by truck to Aalsmeer. Moves were always by night. The total officer complement at Aalsmeer was 17. There were seven Americans, three other Englishmen, a Dutchman, a Frenchman, two Poles and two Canadians, mostly pilots. I do not have an accurate record of the dates, but it is my impression that we moved from Aalsmeer about April 30, and travelled through the night to Huisduinen (Den Helder). Here we were handed over to the German Navy, and lived deep in the bowels of the earth adjacent to the submarine pens. I seem to remember that we were here for about five days, living like moles, and coming up for sunshine and air a couple of hours a day.

Then one afternoon, I imagine it was about May 6, 16 of us were put on a boat, leaving our senior officer, Brigadier-General Bartlett, to fate unknown, and headed out to the north-east and what we knew damn well were minefields. Just before dawn we went ashore at what we found later was Terschelling Island. We did learn later that the intention was to take us to Borkum by one or two night stages. Fortunately we never made it, and I say fortunately because we understand that on May 9/10 all the prisoners at Borkum were shot.

I suppose that in the three days we were on the island we made sufficient nuisance of ourselves to exhaust the patience of the German Captain. We were first moved into the hotel, after living on the beach overnight, and finally to cut a long story short, on condition we gave an undertaking as gentlemen to absolve the German Navy of any responsibility, we were supplied with a German E-boat, an Ensign, two crew and put overboard off the Dutch mainland. By devious means and various routes we all eventually found our way back to England.

The report of the Constable of Government Police follows overleaf.

"Report re an Allied plane, crashed in Maurik on Sunday, April 22nd, 1945.

"On a Sun- or Holy-day in the second part of April 1945 – an investigation proved that April 22nd, 1945 was a Sunday – I was in an house between the villages Maurik and Rijswijk, when I was told that a low flying plane was approaching.

"Owing to the fact that we had no more seen any German plane for months and the allied planes were always flying on safer heights, there was a great interest, as well from the public as from the soldiers of the German Wehrmacht, who were quartered in the neighbourhood.

"I then saw that apparently an allied bomber came flying from north-east and I got the impression that the plane had been shot already as it was flying very low. However, I did not understand why the pilot was flying south-west, as by crossing south the plane would have been above allied territory within 10 kilometres distance.

"When the plane, which flied in the produced part of the river the Rhine, had passed me, the anti-aircraft guns of the Germans, placed in Rijswijk near the canal-bridge and in Wijk bij Duurstede near the ferry, opened a violent fire on the plane. Suddenly the plane turned south and thereafter I saw a parachute hanging in the air. In the meantime the plane returned and came in my direction again. Apparently it had been shot by the anti-aircraft guns, the low flying colossus being an easy prey for same.

"The plane lost rapidly height and flied towards me.

Thundering, roaring and raging it made a last turn in southern direction and at a distance of about 400 metres from me it came down in a meadow, where it got fire.

"Weaponed German soldiers and a numerous public ran to that place. While it was then better for me not to draw the public attention to my person, I looked after the parachute. I saw lowering same slowly, drifting away in south-eastern direction, where it disappeared behind an orchard.

"The plane having burnt out after about half an hour, the Germans released the spot and the carbonized wreckage. Later on that evening I was informed that there had been no crew in the plane anymore. It was said that the plane had been shot already above Germany and that the crew had then left the machine, one pilot excepted. This pilot would have landed just over the new canal from Tiel till Wijk bij Duurstede at the frontier of the municipality Maurik, within the municipality Zoelen. The distance between these two 'landing places' is 3 till 4 kilometres.

"Of the plane, the parts of which were spreaded over a distance of more than 100 metres, there is no more remained than some carbonized parts. Everybody tried to get hold of such a part for souvenir, a bolt or another piece of metal being sufficient already.

"The spot where the plane crashed is very well visible, the more so as there are still lying remainders of the plane there.

"Lienden, May 26th, 1947.
"The Constable of Government Police,
(De Wachtmeester der Rijkspolitie)
w.g. Th. W. v. Schaik."

EN ROUTE – LOW LEVEL *Low flying over the sea could be very exacting. On a calm sunny day the surface would shimmer, with a veil of haze on the horizon, while at night it tended to have a mirror effect and the slightest lapse of concentration could send the props churning up the spray. Tail trimmers would be set well back. Part of the 94-strong force (under the appropriate code name Operation 'Robinson') is seen over the Bay of Biscay en route to the Schneider Armament works at Le Creusot near the French-Swiss Border, for the daring dusk attack of October 17, 1942. In the foreground is the 106 Squadron contingent, ZN-P being an old warrior and still having the unfaired mid-upper turret of only the very earliest Lancs delivered.*

ALL EYES PEELED *An unusual view from the astrodome looking forward, with the D/F (direction-finding) loop in the foreground.*

TUCKING WELL IN *Keeping it tight, F/O J. Rosanski, pilot of BI LL807, 'N-Nuts' of 300 'Masovian' Squadron from Faldingworth, tucks in close en route to the target in the spring of 1944 (below).*

Unique in being the only Polish Lancaster squadron, 300 set up a magnificent record despite high losses and left an indelible name in the annals of Bomber Command. A small replica of the Polish Air Force red and white insignia appears on the nose.

THE SKY IS A BIG PLACE
Looking like a stream of black ants over solid 10/10ths cloud, Lancs from 106 Squadron, Metheringham, on their way to a target early in 1945.

The sky may appear empty but the allied fighter umbrella is there, weaving contrails high above the gaggle.

THE SKY WAS FULL OF 'EM
Lancasters on a mass 'daylight' in support of the allied armies in France in the summer of 1944.

OVER ENEMY TERRITORY
Mouths run dry and that 'butterflies' feeling increases as the target draws near.

The first puffs of flak appear as 75 and 90 Squadrons hold formation over France on a 'daylight' in July 1944.

WINDOW DROPPING *In a sky dotted with flak puffs, a mixed force of Lancs and Halifaxes emerge from a drifting cloud of tinfoil or 'window', used to baffle enemy radar.*

ON TARGET

HAMBURG BY NIGHT *Photography at night was not easy but with the introduction of the photoflash, pictures like these became possible. At 18,000 feet the camera in another kite catches a Lanc over Hamburg on January 30/31, 1943. On this night the weather took a hand, when one of the worst gales for many years raged over the North Sea. This was also the first occasion H2S was used operationally, not by Lancs but by PFF Stirlings and Halifaxes.*

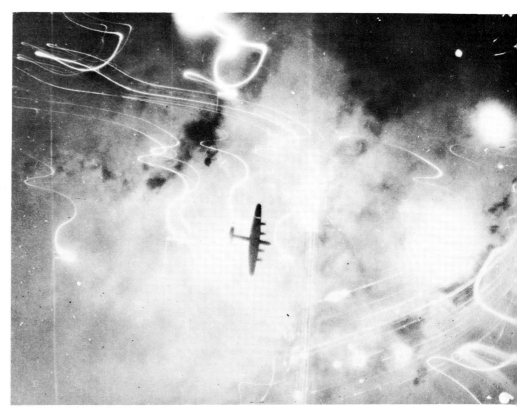

PHOTOFLASH *A confusion of lights, fires, markers, bursting 'cookies', flak and smoke over Pforzheim, February 23/24, 1945. The streets and buildings are briefly revealed as a photoflash lights up the sky and ground. A Lancaster is just visible several thousand feet below.*

BURNING CITY *A Lancaster is silhouetted over Hanover on the night of October 8/9, 1943. The Sallstrasse is clearly highlighted, running diagonally across the picture. A force of 500 Lancasters could drop over 3,000 tons of bombs in a matter of minutes.*

Lightning strike

related by Bill Breckenridge and W. B. ('Biff') Baker

By far the greatest menace on night operations was the enemy night fighter. High in the sub-zero blackness brave young men fought out duels to the death, neither side giving, nor expecting, any quarter. As the RAF fighter pilots had fought so determinedly over Britain in 1940, so did the Luftwaffe night fighter crews fight to save their homeland.

Equipped with only .303 machine guns, our bombers faced the 30mm and 20mm cannon and 7.9mm machine guns of their adversaries – twin-engined Bf110s and Ju88s in the main, but later joined by Do217s, He219s and single-engined Bf109s and Fw190s.

On paper the bomber force stood little chance, but it was argued that, while some would fall to fighters and flak, the sky was a big place and most would get through undetected.

It was a long and bitter struggle, the balance swinging to and fro with constantly changing tactics, ruses and diversions.

Life or death often depended on the keen eyes of the bomber crew, particularly the gunners, who, even in ideal weather conditions, could see no further than 300 yards or so. If visibility was poor, the lurking fighter could suddenly appear, a mere 50 yards away, with all guns blazing, raking the hapless aircraft from stem to stern with devastating effect and giving the crew little chance.

However, by good crew co-ordination, evasive action could be taken and many a crew owed their lives to the famous 'corkscrew' in which the gunners yelled instructions to the pilot, who then threw the kite about the sky, diving and twisting to a set pattern.

Even if the fighter was not seen in time, quick reactions could still save the day. The story below illustrates a grim combat combining superb skill, gallantry and tenacity – plus the necessary element of luck – of a typical well-drilled RAF crew.

As P/O Bill Breckenridge of 626 Squadron and his crew set course for Berlin in Lancaster BI, ME584 UM-Y^2, in the gathering dusk of January 30, 1944, a life-and-death struggle lay but a few hours ahead.

The crew comprised three Scotsmen, three Canadians and an Englishman. This was their sixth trip together

BOMB DOORS OPEN *With doors agape, BI, LL783, C-Charlie of 619 Squadron, Coningsby, shows to advantage its capacious bomb bay – 33 feet long and almost half the fuselage length.*

and already they had been to Berlin three times, besides Brunswick and Magdeburg for variety.

It was a pleasant evening with little cloud, which suited the Canadian navigator, Jack Meek. He was able to get several accurate winds with their direction and strength.

They had no trouble getting to the target. Some combats were seen as they came in from the north and swung in, well on time, at 20,000 feet, with the moon above on the starboard side. There was plenty of flak and the low clouds, with tops to about 8,000 feet, were lit up by searchlights.

They had settled on the bombing run when suddenly an unseen fighter attacked at close range, perhaps 200 yards, on the starboard side. The kite shuddered as shells tore into the metal, making a terrific din, so loud it could be heard above the engines.

The mid-upper turret was smashed and 'Biff' Baker, the Englishman, a keen amateur boxer, was hit on the side of his face, his helmet and oxygen mask torn away. The rear turret was badly holed and the Canadian, Joe Schwartz, severely wounded by a piece of exploding shrapnel in his foot. Both he and 'Biff' Baker soon lapsed into unconsciousness. The intercom to the rear end was u/s so those forward did not know what was happening aft.

Bill, the skipper, took immediate evasive action, diving to starboard. On recovering, he again levelled out on the bombing run and Val Poushinsky, the Canadian bomb aimer, dropped the load on the estimated position of the markers seen before the attack.

A minute later they were again attacked, perhaps by the same fighter, but this time from the port quarter, and at 400 yards. With his two gunners out cold, though he did not know it, the skipper had no warning but dived to port on observing the first tracers coming in.

The kite was pitching around all over the place as the skipper tried everything he knew to shake off the fighter. The navigator, crouched down behind the skipper, was doubled up from hits and instinctively grabbed his chute before passing out.

Things were certainly happening fast. They could not shake off the searchlights or flak, let alone the fighter. It was a madhouse, with the terrific noise of exploding shells and screaming engines.

After a further two minutes, the fighter found them again. He closed in from the starboard quarter, at 400 yards, and let forth yet another devastating barrage. This time the skipper was hit, a passing bullet grazing his legs.

The original course was resumed from the target

BOMBS GONE *A load of 1,000-pounders drops away between the flak bursts, as Lancs and Halifaxes bomb enemy troop concentrations after D-Day.*

area after further violent manœuvres, but three minutes later came the fourth attack. Again they were hit but the range was now about 500 yards.

By the time the fighter was shaken off, their height was down to 15,000 feet. No further attacks came as the skipper, completely unflurried and flying his battered kite as if on a cross-country trip, got away from the area as fast as possible.

Slowly the crew began to recover. Jimmy, the wireless op, was found slumped over his set. He was warm but unconscious, so he was given first aid. Not until they landed would they know he was past help.

Jack Meek regained consciousness to discover that he had two wounds. One was in his shoulder. The other was caused by shrapnel which went clean through his middle, entering at the right side of his back and emerging at the left front, just below his chest, missing his heart by inches. Though he knew he was badly hit, he would not know the full extent of his injuries until they landed.

'Biff' Baker and Joe Schwartz also revived. The latter extricated himself from his turret, crawled up the fuselage to the rest-bed, but again collapsed. Val Poushinsky rendered first aid to both Schwartz and Meek before taking up a position in the astrodome. Meanwhile, 'Biff' Baker clambered into the still-

serviceable rear turret, even though he was injured and without oxygen.

To make matters worse, the rear fuselage began to fill with smoke soon after leaving the target area. Alex Stephenson, the engineer, went aft and put out the fire.

The kite was in a fearful state. The hydraulic system had been shot away. The bomb doors would not close, nor, as they found later, would the wheels lower. One petrol tank was holed, three rev counters and three boost gauges useless, as were the direction finder and gyro-compass. The elevators and rudders were also badly damaged.

Jack Meek's navigational gear was wrecked, but the accurate data on the winds on the route-in now came in handy. All he could do was dead reckon on these, but in reverse. He could not hold up the sextant for his left arm kept dropping down, finally becoming completely useless.

Luckily, his figures were good for they took them right back on track. He also took observation of landmarks he knew. When he saw searchlights or flak over German territory he would say to the skipper, "That's Hanover. Go so many minutes in such a direction then bear so much west." Two hours after leaving Berlin he was able to get a Gee fix despite feeling lightheaded from loss of blood and lack of oxygen. They were now

over the Zuider Zee and only three miles off track.

The open bomb doors caused a lot of drag and the skipper could not get much speed, though he did manage to hold altitude. All were chilled through, due to the many gaping holes, while the lack of oxygen was taking its toll.

Over the North Sea the electrical system caught fire, but the mid-upper and flight engineer succeeded in extinguishing the fire after a short, fierce battle.

Thirty miles from the English coast the Gee packed up. A distress signal was sent out and in less than a minute the searchlights were homing them in to Docking, on the Norfolk coast. A crash-landing was inevitable. The wheels would not come down, as the air pressure was blown away, and frantic efforts by the skipper and engineer resisted all attempts to unlock them.

With the crew at crash positions, the skipper brought the kite in, but she was difficult to control and he had to overshoot. On the second attempt he brought her in like a baby, ran forward on the tailwheel, nose well up, then slowed. The open bomb doors hit the ground, snapped shut, and suddenly all was quiet. They were down. There was no fire.

BIRD'S-EYE VIEW *of a Lanc BX,* KB745 *VR-V, of 419 'Moose' Squadron, RCAF, skippered by F/O A. C. Rokeby, RCAF, gracefully silhouetted over the remains of a flying bomb site in the summer of 1944. In this fine picture, the dinghy stowage is clearly outlined in the starboard wing. This Lanc was almost new at the time, and the glossier finish of the Canadian-built machines is still relatively fresh.*

KRUPPS OF ESSEN *Words which struck a cold chill when announced at briefing. No target in Germany was more vital; none was more heavily defended. Although frequently pounded by Bomber Command it was mid-1944 before any real impression began to be made, so fiercely did the Germans fight to preserve the country's major armaments-producing complex.*

BOMBS AWAY *"Steady, steady, left – left, steady, bombs gone, bomb doors closed." The skipper of this 49 Squadron Lanc from Fulbeck will be holding her steady for the aiming point photograph as the 1,000-pounders hurtle downwards on to an already doomed V-site in France.*

Daylight sorties by Lancs on Germany alone totalled 23,204 for the loss of only 179, such was the allied domination of the air.

84

THE DESOLATION OF WAR
Not a chimney; not a roof; not a building untouched; the destruction almost complete. A tragic scene so typical in the industrial Ruhr which received the constant and unerring attention of Bomber Command. This picture of Wesel was taken soon after the war's close, from the rear turret of a Lancaster carrying ground crew on a 4-hour "Cooks Tour" of places which had hitherto been distant names to them.

PLASTERED *All that remained of the V1 site at Siracourt in the Pas-de-Calais following the Canadian 6 Group attack of July 6, 1944. The Allies waged a massive and prolonged campaign, code-named Noball, against the V1 and V2 sites, which reached its peak in July and August 1944. The brunt of the attacks fell on Bomber Command, the Lancaster squadrons in particular, and in a 53-day period, 179 separate attacks were made, involving well over 10,000 sorties. Such was the intensity of operations in this period that a Lanc crew could complete a tour in three months.*

THE WAY BACK

HEADING FOR HOME *Dusk gathers as a G-H leader from 195 Squadron, Wratting Common, nears the English coast on return from an attack on Dortmund, March 12, 1945. This picture was taken by the navigator of another kite in the 'vic'.*

On this raid two Bomber Command records were set: 1,107 aircraft participated, dropping 4,851 tons – the highest number of aircraft and highest tonnage respectively on one target.

THE LAST SECONDS *as flak claims another victim, a kite from 75 'New Zealand' Squadron, Mepal, on the edge of the stream, shudders as she is hit by a direct burst over France in July 1944. A few seconds later she disintegrated.*

The Cathedral and I survived

Fred Smooker

Fate moves in mysterious ways. Many men alive today still wonder why they were singled out for survival while their comrades perished.

Most have no idea how they escaped from their stricken Lancaster and, try as they might, there is an unaccountable gap in their lives, varying from several minutes to an hour or more.

If the aircraft received a direct hit from flak, there was little chance of anyone surviving, save perhaps the pilot if he was wearing a seat-type chute (standard issue by 1944 and later extended to rear gunners). He alone might find himself floating to earth, hanging from a tree, lying in a field or snowdrift, badly shaken but alive, not quite knowing how or why.

Flak or fighters might wreck the bomber or set it on fire, giving the crew some chance of donning their parachutes. However, if the kite went into an uncontrollable dive or spin, none could move, let alone escape, due to terrific centrifugal forces, but one could still be thrown out, perhaps as the aircraft exploded.

Others were thrown clear in crashes, ending up in such unlikely places as haystacks, pigsties, mudflats, or crashing through the roof of a building – sometimes receiving no more than a few scratches and bruises.

When, in the early hours of July 10, 1943, Lancaster BIII, ED720 ZN-R, of 106 Squadron, Syerston, exploded near Cambrai while returning from Cologne, only the bomb aimer was destined to live. As this account reveals, his experiences left an indelible impression on his mind.

Our American pilot, F/O Gene Rosner, was in the RCAF and had returned us safely from some eighteen operations, the last one being on Cologne on June 28, 1943.

After this operation we were due for some leave – aircrew in those days were given nine days' leave every six weeks.

Following interrogation after our Cologne trip and a bacon and egg breakfast, we all tidied up and headed our separate ways to wherever we spent our leave.

On returning a week later, our skipper, who had on numerous occasions been pestering the USAAF authorities to accept him into their ranks, told us he would be returning to London to remuster, and that he would try to get us some more leave while he was away.

On his return from London two days later, he was wearing the olive green outfit of an American First Lieutenant. He had been accepted by his own mob but was to complete his tour of operations with the RAF. Somehow, he was now a stranger to me, and to crown all, operations that night were again on Cologne, and we were to take along a second dickey pilot for experience before he took his own crew on ops. It was his first op.

The met. men told us there would be cumulonimbus clouds up to 20,000 feet over the target. We would not be worried by fighters, because they would be grounded. It was to be an all-Lancaster effort, 'Wanganui' type, bombing through ten-tenths cloud.

There were two types of bombing those days, 'Paramatta' and 'Wanganui'. For 'Paramatta' the Pathfinders laid coloured markers on the ground; red in the middle, surrounded by green, and bomb aimers aimed at the patchwork of red and green markers on the ground. The 'Wanganui' type was used when the target was covered by cloud. The Pathfinders dropped first a white parachute flare which we had to track over and alter course for the target area. Next came a green flare, over which we had to track because it was the run-in to the target which was indicated by a final red flare. Using special settings on the bombsight, bomb aimers had to aim at this red flare. This method was said to be more accurate than visual ground bombing, and that we could obliterate one square mile of target area by such concentration. To me, this type of bombing was also more dangerous, because the Germans knew the height of clouds, and they knew the Lancasters' ceiling, hence all flak was concentrated accordingly.

Our trip over the North Sea was uneventful and, sure enough, over the Belgian coast we were over the clouds, as forecast.

The white flare was dropped at some point north of Cologne where we turned south for the target. Then things began to happen. Searchlights turned the clouds into a dazzling white sea of snow. We began to see that we were not alone on our journey of destruction; in front and to either side could be seen the black silhouettes of our accompanying Lancasters, from whom no help was possible in the event of disaster. The sea of dazzling white was now beginning to be splashed with jagged cherry-red flashes which disintegrated into red-hot coals. The green flare appeared directly ahead. We were right on track and so was the flak. The jagged flashes were now all around us, and I could feel my inside begin its usual churning and my flesh and skin begin to tighten, whilst all my instincts told me to cringe and curl up into a ball.

The red flare appeared ahead; the pilot told me our airspeed and altitude over the intercom, while I busied myself setting the special adjustments to the bombsight.

By now we had ceased our continuous climbing and diving, weaving to port and starboard, and were flying straight and level over a white shiny carpet mottled with an angry red glow. One felt that one could get out and walk on it.

On my instructions, the bomb doors were opened to expose to the hail of red-hot metal being thrown at us, some five tons of high explosive and incendiary bombs. It seemed an eternity before the red flare came into my sights and I literally screamed, "Bombs gone."

Our Lancaster leapt a thousand feet higher on being released from the load in her belly. Within seconds we had the bomb doors closed, and our skipper again started our Lanc doing its jigging and weaving as if our lives depended upon it – which they did.

As we continued south, the worst of the holocaust was beginning to retreat behind us, and my taut nerves began to unwind as my brain told my organs to stop pumping adrenalin into my bloodstream.

"Keep a lookout for fighters," called the skipper to the gunners and myself, who was also front gunner, so I lay on my stomach in the bomb bay, gazing out of my huge Perspex dome.

When we reached a point on our south track, we turned on a westerly course for home, as plotted by our navigator. We were at some 22,000 feet. "Hello, skipper," called Ted Amor, our flight engineer. "The starboard outer is heating up."

"OK, Ted, keep an eye on it."

Minutes later, "Hello, skipper, the starboard outer temperature is worse and still climbing."

"OK, Ted, we'll have to feather the prop. Stop the engine and fly on three." After a while on three engines, the inside temperature of the plane became extremely low, and I found that one of my feet had numbed with the cold. Crouching in my bombing compartment I slipped off my boot and massaged my foot back to life.

"Hey, you guys," called the skipper. "I'm going to fly straight and level to keep up with the concentration." This concentration, although invisible, consisted of 200-odd other Lancs carrying out the same tactics as ourselves and, to prevent the German defences pinpointing on individuals, we all flew more or less at the same height and airspeed, but with our having only three engines our airspeed had dropped.

"Hey, bomb aimer," called our skipper. "Can you get at my feet and give them a massage?" Of course I could if I stood up in my compartment, his feet on the rudders being just at my shoulder height. I pulled on my left boot, and commenced my massaging operation on the skipper's feet. His feet were more important than mine in this position.

However, after five minutes or so, my own left foot was again numb, so I asked Ted Amor if he would come and take over the task of rubbing heat into the skipper's feet while I attended to my own. I think the skipper and I must have had damp socks, because no one else complained.

While Ted was doing his stuff on the skipper's foot, and I had my left boot off, rubbing my own foot, there was a terrific sickening crash. The Perspex dome in the nose disintegrated and a blast of ice-cold air gushed into my compartment where target maps and other sundry items started swirling about the place.

"There's a fighter!" yelled Jim Calder, our Canadian mid-upper gunner. I scrambled up into my front gun-turret but the controls were dead. I was helpless.

"The starboard inner's on fire," yelled Jim Calder.

"OK, Ted," said the skipper to the engineer. "Get back up here."

"Turn to port," yelled Jim Calder. Ted Amor went back to his position alongside the skipper, when I think they feathered the starboard inner also, but suddenly our two port engines, I assume, started to speed up in an increasing crescendo until they were almost screaming.

Over the intercom came the skipper's voice. "Hey, you guys, we gotta bale out. Somebody get me my parachute. Bale out, bale out, bale out. . . ."

Our two screaming port engines suddenly stopped dead, and then came the most sickening of sensations – falling like a stone out of the sky in a dead aeroplane. I couldn't believe it even as I grabbed my chute and clipped it on. It was impossible! It couldn't be happening! I pulled at the handle of my escape hatch upon which a few minutes ago I had been squatting, massaging my left foot. The square hatch had wedged itself across the hole, and when kicking it free I realised I still had only one boot on.

Even then I was expecting the engines to restart. I didn't want to bale out, but to stay meant death. Gripping my ripcord handle in my right hand, I went feet first into the gaping hole in the floor. My legs were swept under the belly of the Lanc; away went my one remaining boot. My Mae West, which had inflated inadvertently, had me fast in the hole. I wriggled out like a woman wriggles out of a corset; with one hand still on my ripcord handle I was out. I didn't count ten – I pulled. I felt the plane pass over me, then I was whirling in space, cringing as if expecting a sudden violent shock which would jar the life out of me.

The sudden shock came, but I was still alive, although I had a burning pain in my groin. I was hanging in my parachute. Very gingerly I reached up both hands to grasp my shoulder straps and ease the weight off my groin. The chute gave a lurch and my heart almost stopped, then thud, I was on my back on terra firma, looking up at my parachute canopy slowly collapsing on to the ground in front of me.

I stood up, and immediately my legs gave way. My two ankles were lifeless. "God," I thought, "my ankles are broken." Some 500 yards away in the distance there was a terrific fire, crackling like a Browning machine-gun pouring out some 1,200 rounds a minute. My Lancaster, I guessed. Then came the awful doubt that surely no one else could have got out in time.

Overhead, a continuous droning of Lancasters. Come and get me I prayed, then reason returned. Hide your parachute and get away from your aircraft as fast as possible. I got to my feet again and this time stayed upright. Thank God, my ankles can't be broken, only sprained. Hobbling about I bundled up my parachute into a ball, but where to hide it, as I was in a field? Pulling up some long grass, I laid the chute in a hollow and covered it with grass. Not very well hidden, but I was going to have enough to do to walk, without lugging a parachute with me until I found a good hiding place.

Get away from the plane. I hobbled over the fields in my socks, gasping with pain as I went, until all was quiet – no burning Lancaster, no droning Lancasters overhead, only me in a field in France at about 03.30 hrs on July 10, 1943.

I was not caught by the Germans until after mid-September, and did not arrive in a PoW camp until about November 15. For 56 days I was held in solitary confinement in a Paris prison, but that is another story.

On my release from PoW camp in May 1945, the Americans flew us from Halle to Brussels, and for some reason we flew over Cologne. I know it was Cologne I was looking at out of the window of the Dakota because I was astounded to see the huge Cathedral, apparently unscathed, towering up out of a scene of utter devastation.

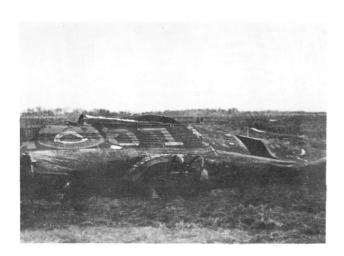

THREE OF OUR AIRCRAFT FAILED TO RETURN *Bomber Command paid a high price for its sustained offensive. The cost in lives was 47,000 aircrew killed (which represents 67 per cent of the total RAF casualties or 12 per cent of Britain's total service and civilian casualties).*

3,349 Lancasters failed to return

from operations. Offset against this, they completed 156,308 sorties, almost half the total sorties of Bomber Command. These are the remains (above left) at NW Sch. Berle in Holland of pathfinder BIII, JB280 LQ-K, of 405 'Vancouver' Squadron RCAF from Gransden Lodge, shot down on a Berlin trip on the night of January 1/2, 1944.

The wreckage (above) of BIII, JB601 ZN-V from 106 Squadron, Metheringham, lying near Laneuville-a-Bayard in the Forêt-du-Val on the Swiss/French border, caught by a Bf109 on the way to Schweinfurt April 26/27, 1944.

First light would find investigation teams scouring the countryside for the twisted wreckage of aircraft brought down during the night.

The morbid task of sifting through the sorry remains would begin, in the hope of gleaning anything useful to German Intelligence.

Often, little was left, and this Lancaster, brought down by flak over the Dutch coast in May 1943, would reveal little of value. To this day it remains unidentified.

DOWN IN THE DRINK *Ditching at night could be a particularly hazardous experience, especially when the aircraft was badly damaged. Often it was a case of a few precious minutes before she sank, calling for a high degree of efficiency and thorough acquaintance with each stage of the ditching procedure and dinghy drill.*

In favourable circumstances, however, some Lancs stayed afloat for many hours and here is a BI, W4318 PM-C, which remained afloat for 33 hours.

On the night of April 13/14, 1943, Sgt Johnny Stoneman and crew of 103 Squadron ran out of petrol over the Channel on the way back from Spezia in Italy. Visibility was clear and the sea calm, apart from a slight swell. Approaching the water at 100 mph, with 20° of flap and all engines serviceable, the skipper ditched in an 85 mph glide, alighting along the crest of the swell.

The first impact was moderate, the second slight and the whole crew immediately took to the dinghy. After 3½ hours they were rescued by a Walrus and Air Sea Rescue launch. Being still afloat at daylight, an attempt at salvage was made and a ship tried to tow her into port. Getting too close, the ship chopped off her tail, when she tipped up on her nose and sank, 50 miles off Falmouth.

Seven more for the Goldfish Club

John Goldsmith

No crew relished the thought of ditching in the cold, unfriendly sea. It was difficult enough to judge the swell in daylight, but at night it was even more hazardous.

A successful ditching demanded a high degree of skill on the part of the pilot and, once in the water, efficient crew drill was essential if they were to get clear of the sinking plane. It was to prepare crews for such an event that mock 'dry-land' ditchings were practised regularly.

Once in the dinghy their adventures really began. Rescue could be within a few hours in clear weather, but in heavy seas or misty conditions they could drift helplessly for days and quickly become victims of exposure.

If they were unfortunate enough to ditch near the enemy coast, a German rescue launch might reach them first, and the thought of spending the remainder of the war behind barbed wire was a gloomy prospect.

F/Lt Bob Etchells of 156 Squadron brought off a textbook ditching in his Lancaster BIII, PB302 GT-B, in the early hours of August 27, 1944. F/Lt Johnny Goldsmith, his Canadian navigator, wrote the following account a few days later while the event was still fresh in his mind.

In the afternoon of August 26, 1944, I was asked to fly with F/Lt Etchells, as his navigator was sick. It was my first bombing operation that month, and I was glad of the opportunity to get in a little action. I was duty navigator that day, and I knew quite early that the target was Kiel, a very heavily defended target; but as most of the route was over water it seemed to be a pretty good trip. Take-off was at 20.00 hrs, so we were well over the North Sea by dusk. We were on track all the way to the target, and on time to within 10 seconds. The bombing run at 22,000 feet was good, although a slight overshoot, so we withheld our target markers but let the bombs go. A split second after the bomb aimer said, "Bombs away," the rear gunner yelled, "Enemy fighter astern. Corkscrew port." The fighter and our gunner opened fire practically simultaneously, opening range being about 300 yards. The rear gunner reported hits scored on the enemy fighter, a Junkers 88, and it was last seen falling away with flames coming from a position between its port engine and fuselage. The rear gunner claimed it as probably destroyed.

Our aircraft was hit in a number of places, and the damage was as follows: starboard outer propeller shot off, starboard inner engine hit and on fire – so the engine was stopped and propeller feathered, and the fire went out. Port tail assembly pretty well shot away.

Front of rear turret smashed, a two-foot square hole in the bottom of the fuselage near the tail turret, caused when one cannon shell exploded inside the fuselage near tail turret. Most of my navigation instruments made unserviceable, so I navigated to the North Sea by dead reckoning. As we still had the target markers, we decided to jettison them in the sea as it would be very dangerous to attempt a landing with them still on board. After jettisoning we found that the bomb doors could not be closed, also the port wheel had come down and could not be retracted. About an hour after leaving the target, the port inner engine caught fire, and we began losing altitude about 150 feet per minute, so 'ditching' was inevitable.

I figured our position at that time to be about 160 miles from England and 50 miles north of the Frisian Islands, held by Germany. This position was given to the wireless operator, but he could not get it off as an SOS because the fixed aerial was shot away and the trailing aerial was earthed on the open bomb doors. We were losing height rapidly, so crash positions were taken. Under the circumstances I doubt if any of the crew expected to live long. I know I didn't. Owing to the darkness and mist, it was almost impossible to see the water. We hit it nose first with a sudden smash, and the aircraft slid along for a short distance on its belly. The racket was terrible, and water was flying everywhere. We came to a stop with the nose under water, which seemed to be coming in everywhere.

Dinghy drill was carried out very well, and we all got out on the wing OK. The dinghy inflated all right, but we had difficulty getting it off the wing and into the water, as the wing was on a slant with the trailing edge in the air. We finally managed to get it into the water but found that it was under the tail, and it appeared that the aircraft would go under at any moment and take us with it. Three of us jumped into the water and started swimming with the dinghy in tow and, together with the aid of the others who were paddling, we finally got it away from the aircraft, which sank in a very short time. The estimated time the aircraft stayed afloat was about four minutes.

Now that we were safely down and into the dinghy, we began to take stock of the situation. It was still hard to believe that after all we'd been through we were still alive; in fact none of us was injured. At the time the sea was fairly calm, and I guess that was the main reason we were still alive. Our dinghy radio had been washed away, so there we were, in the middle of the North Sea and, as far as we knew, not a soul other than ourselves knew it. Things looked pretty black, but we had a good supply of water and emergency rations which we intended to make last for seven days. At the end of that time, if we were not found we figured we never would be. Most important of all we had a Very light pistol and about two dozen red flares. Helmets and boots were thrown overboard since there was some danger of their fittings puncturing the rubber dinghy. We decided to put out the sea anchor and wait until daylight before trying to paddle.

About 02.00 hrs we heard an aircraft approaching very low, and we fired off two red flares when he was overhead. The aircraft turned and circled and dropped a white flare, lighting us up, then proceeded on course. This cheered us up a great deal, and it seemed a wonderful bit of luck that we should be sighted so soon. During the next few hours we heard other aircraft, but none came close. Then, about 05.00 hrs, a Lancaster flew over low, and we fired off more red flares. He circled us four times, flashed OK on his downward identification light and left. By this time we were sure of being picked up soon; it just seemed a matter of time. Occasionally we could see searchlights on the German coast, and we had visions of ending up as prisoners of war.

Daylight finally came, and we started to paddle towards England, steering by small compasses we all carried. After about half an hour we realised how hopeless it was. The dinghy was round, and all we seemed to do was drift around in circles, so we finally gave it up as a bad job.

About 11.00 hrs that morning we heard aircraft, but visibility was very poor, and we were doubtful whether they'd see us. After half an hour we saw three Air Sea Rescue Hudsons patrolling about five miles away. We fired off red flares, but they were too far away to see them and they disappeared in the fog. About ten minutes later they came back, this time closer, and we fired off more red flares; but it looked as though they still hadn't seen us, when suddenly the first one turned and came directly towards us flying very low and followed by the other two. They circled us and dropped smoke floats to get a drift in preparation for dropping an airborne lifeboat. Finally one Hudson flew over at about 800 feet, and we saw the boat fall out and parachute to the sea, the idea being to drop downwind. A sea anchor would shoot out and anchor it, and we were supposed to drift into it. However, the mechanism which was supposed to shoot out the sea anchor didn't work, and the lifeboat drifted away from us, though we paddled furiously. We certainly felt low just sitting there unable to do anything and watching it drift away. Another thing, our dinghy was leaking and we had no bellows to blow it up; so things really looked bad.

A short time later another of the Hudsons flew over and dropped us a Lindholme dinghy which consists of another rubber dinghy and four containers holding emergency rations, water and flares. This was a very good drop, and we drifted on to it about 10 minutes afterwards. For a while it looked as though we were going to miss it, so we fastened a rope to the rear gunner who jumped into the water and tried to swim to it; but after four minutes he was exhausted trying to swim as the water was cold and very rough. He was practically unconscious when we pulled him back into the dinghy and it took quite a while to bring him round. This proved to us that if we fell out of the dinghy and drifted away, there was little chance of survival.

We tied the Lindholme dinghy to our own so that we were about 10 feet apart and, with sea anchors out, lessened the chances of one of the dinghies capsizing. The pilot, engineer and myself transferred to the other dinghy, as it was almost impossible to move with the seven of us in one. During the rest of the day there was at least one Hudson circling us. Towards late afternoon, the sky was overcast and the sea got rougher, and we were all soaked and miserably cold. It was impossible to keep the dinghy dry inside, so we were always sitting in water.

Towards dusk another Hudson appeared with an airborne lifeboat which was dropped fairly close, but it became dark before we could reach it. We stayed awake all the time because the sea was so rough we were afraid we might capsize at any time, and also we had to keep baling the water out of the dinghy.

Shortly after midnight the moon broke through the clouds. It was a beautiful sight and cheered us considerably. We soon saw the lifeboat. This time it was fairly close, and a few hours later we managed to reach it. It certainly felt good to get into it at last. There were seven dry waterproof suits in the lockers of the boat, which is about the same size as a large rowboat. We changed into these and threw our clothes into the sea as there was no room on the boat for them. As I was the only one who knew anything about boats I was elected to run it. I decided to wait until daylight, until the Air Sea Rescue Hudsons came out to us again. At 08.00 hrs the first Hudson appeared. We found out later that about this time a Junkers 88 was circling only a mile away, apparently looking for us, but it disappeared when the Hudsons closed in on it.

We got everything ship-shape on the boat, the two four-horsepower outboard engines were started, and we set course for England. After an hour the sea became so rough that the motors were swamped, and we couldn't get them started again. It was hopeless putting up the sail as a real northerly gale was blowing. It is estimated that the wind had a force of 30 to 40 knots, and the seas were mountainous.

The boat had been damaged when it hit the water and now, under the battering of the heavy seas, it began to break up and leak badly. By about 14.00 hrs the boat was almost completely awash and was held afloat only by the rubber buoyancy chambers lining the sides of the deck and the bow and stern. Practically everything was washed overboard. We had finally given up hope of being saved, and most of us were praying hard. It was decided that, as a last resort when the boat broke up, we would tie ourselves together and with our Mae Wests on would float as long as possible, although we didn't expect to survive long in the heavy seas. Two Hudsons were still circling at this time, but their efforts seemed futile.

About 16.00 hrs, when we had all resigned ourselves to the inevitable, Bob, the pilot, yelled, "A ship!" I didn't believe it at first, but sure enough it was a sailing boat being guided to us by the aircraft. When it got closer we saw that it was a small Danish fishing boat, and I'd say that it was the most beautiful sight I had ever seen or ever will see. It was quite an effort getting us aboard owing to the rough sea, but finally we made it. We were so full of relief we just laid down on the deck for a while trying to realise how lucky we were.

After a while we began to consider the situation. Here we were on a Danish fishing boat heading for where, we didn't know, but even a prisoner of war camp would have looked better to us than remaining in what was left of the lifeboat.

There were four Danes in the crew of the boat, and one fellow had fished out of Grimsby for six years before the war, and he could speak a little English. We asked him where he was going and he replied that he had finished fishing and was on his way to Denmark. Then we asked him to take us to Sweden where we would expect better treatment than from the Germans who would capture us if we went to Denmark, but he said that was impossible. When we said England, he only smiled. About ten minutes later one of the Hudsons flew over and dropped a message container. The message stated, "Steer course 250 degrees for England, good luck." This seemed to worry the Danes and they argued amongst themselves for almost five minutes, then started turning round. One of the boys looked at the compass a while later and saw that we were on a course of 250 degrees, so all looked well. The Danes accepted the situation and took us down to the cabin and lit the stove, and we dried ourselves out and put on dry clothes which they provided. We were told we

could use their bunks, and we were soon fast asleep. I felt better in the morning, but found I was so weak I could hardly stand. The weather was so bad during the night that we had to heave to until daylight.

One of the Danes brought us some food which consisted of canned meat and fish, German bread, which seemed to be half sawdust, and ersatz tea which tasted great to us as it was the first hot drink we'd had, but normally I doubt if I would be able to drink it as it certainly had no resemblance to tea.

During the day we tried to teach the Danes a little English and vice versa. The one fellow who could speak English told us a lot about Denmark and the Germans. They had a very good wireless receiver which they allowed us to use, and we listened to everything from German propaganda broadcasts in English to Bing Crosby. We found it rather amusing watching the Danes shaving off about two weeks' beard and getting all cleaned up for their arrival in England; in fact, when the Air Sea Rescue launch met us they couldn't tell who were Danes and who were English at first.

It was about 17.00 hrs on the 29th that we were met by the rescue launch. They told us they'd been very close to us the day after we'd ditched but lost contact with the aircraft who were circling us. Then one engine broke down, and they had to go back to their base. We were in the Air Sea Rescue launch until after midnight when we were landed in Grimsby, about 80 hours since we had left England. We then went to a Naval hospital where we were given a good meal, and the doctor examined us to see if we were fit. Next night we returned to the squadron, where we were given a great welcome and then went on 14 days' survivors' leave.

HOME ON TWO *Not an unfamiliar sight to returning crews; with two props feathered, BI LM141 of 460 Squadron makes it back to Binbrook after an argument with German flak in the summer of 1944. Some Lancs are known to have made the last lap on one engine, in a long, shallow descent.*

SAFELY HOME

WELCOME SIGHT *One by one the kites return in the early hours and (left) one enters the circuit at East Kirkby as the sun rises over the Windmill at Old Bolingbroke.*

The local farmers and villagers would count them in and hope. . . . The mill. was the home of the Eleys, regular hosts to crews of Nos. 57 and 630 Squadrons.

MISSION COMPLETED *F/Lt Stuart Anning brings BI, ED763 KC-Z Honor, of 617 Squadron, Woodhall Spa, in to land after the third and successful attack on the battleship Tirpitz, November 12, 1944.*

Flying from Lossiemouth to Bals Fjord, Tromso in Norway, the operation involved a round trip of 13 hours. Load was one 12,000lb tallboy.

We "died" three times

Bill Bennée

Some crews could get through a tour with little or no trouble, their gunners never having to fire a shot in anger. For others, it seemed as if the enemy had taken a personal dislike to them. They would return from trip after trip with graphic tales of duels with searchlights, flak or fighters, their aircraft riddled with holes.

Although a tour normally comprised 30 trips, crews would not always know when they were on their last operation because it could vary either way. It depended on the fortunes of the squadron – who may not have had a crew finish for months, the pressing need for instructors, or revised thinking by Bomber Command chiefs.

F/Lt Bill Bennée and crew, of 101 Squadron, Holme-on-Spalding Moor, were somewhat apprehensive when briefed for Munich – always a tough target – on the night of March 9/10, 1943, for they knew it was to be their last trip in their trusty Lanc BI, ED552 SR-Q *Gremlin Queen*.

Any hopes they may have had of their luck lasting out were shattered even before they left the English coast. The following vivid account was written by the skipper shortly after the war.

It would not be difficult for anyone to imagine that after each sortie, climbing out of the aircraft and standing on terra firma was indeed a wonderful sensation. But never before or since have I experienced a greater thrill or feeling of thankfulness than when I did this selfsame thing after completing the last sortie of my first Operational Tour, having escaped death three times on a trip that took just under nine hours.

On that memorable night we were briefed to attack the famous Beer Cellar town of Munich, and ironically enough our first escape was over this country. Subsequently we learned that our demise was nearly brought about by a member of our own squadron!

Some six hundred aircraft were to rendezvous at 18,000 feet over Dungeness, with navigation lights burning, and were in fact all circling round a searchlight beam which was being shown vertically at that point. On receiving word from the navigator, I had just turned the aircraft on to course and, looking up, saw approaching at great speed what appeared to be red balls of fire. No navigation lights were visible but I realised after a little hesitation that I was looking down the flame traps of the exhausts of another aircraft approaching head on, and immediately commenced a steep turn to starboard. My port wing had barely lifted when the other aircraft passed us; it was so close we actually heard its engines. This is no line – all the

crew heard them. Only one other member of the crew saw what I had seen; he was the bomb aimer on look-out in the nose, and by the time he had opened his mouth to give me warning the danger had passed. This indicates how quickly the whole thing happened. Needless to say, the reaction to this narrowly-averted disaster was sudden and violent and I admit that I could not stop myself from trembling for nearly half an hour. Even then I was still shaken, but although I did not know it at the time, further shocks were awaiting me that night.

Over the target area on the bombing run, with three minutes straight run up to the aiming point, we were coned in searchlights. I am not a brave man but there was a certain amount of friendly rivalry on the squadron as to which crew would get the best picture of the aiming point, and as this was our last trip we were determined to get a good picture. With my crew's consent, we pressed on straight and level, taking no evasive action. Jerry was quick to show his appreciation of the 'clot' above in no uncertain manner and we were subjected to intense heavy flak. Our load comprised 30lb incendiaries and a shell splinter set one off. I shall never forget the sight of the bright red glare of the touched-off incendiary mingling with the intense blue-white of some thirty-odd searchlights reflecting through to the bomb aimer's compartment just beyond my feet. However, we carried on, dropped our bombs, did *not* stop to take a picture and turned back steeply to port. Caught on the turn by a heavy flak burst close to its belly, the aircraft stood on its nose and plummeted vertically.

With the airspeed building up rapidly to fighter aircraft proportions, my trim controls jammed and, blinded by the searchlights, we were extremely fortunate that the Lancaster at last responded to her elevators and we pulled out of our dive at over 400 mph. Suddenly we were in complete blackness; I still could not see my instruments after the glare of the searchlights. When I was able to see them, however, I had a further shock. We were at 5,000 feet and there were hills in the vicinity of over 6,000 feet. This we knew although, of course, we could not see them. The gods were certainly good to us that night; we must have pulled out of our dive into a valley. Soon we were back at a reasonable height of 12,000 feet but still climbing and heading for home.

My next worry was how badly the aircraft had been damaged. The controls did not feel too good and it was therefore common sense in one way not to put too much stress on the airframe by unnecessary manoeuvres. On the other hand, by not carrying out a particular manœuvre we laid ourselves open to attack from underneath by night fighters.

The final episode of my story took place a few miles from the French coast, just when we were beginning to feel that this was not a night meant for our destruction and that we stood a reasonable chance of 'making it'.

Out of the blackness, stabs of tracers flew past our starboard wing and in a moment an ugly orange glare lit the sky only 50 yards away. It was sufficient for us to see that it was one of our own four-engined bombers which would not be returning to base. We all stared, fascinated, as the great and beautiful bird born of the scientific genius of man made its death dive to explode some 16,000 feet below to form the funeral pyre of seven brave lads who had 'had their time'.

Such an end was accepted by all crews as a possibility and I must confess that my feelings towards this scene which I had just witnessed were simply that I was glad it wasn't me.

After this I took a certain amount of evasive action until well clear of the coast. On approaching the shores of England the certainty grew stronger that we were not destined for the 'chop' that night. All the same, we did not really relax until we were once again standing on terra firma at our dispersal.

There was an anti-climax to our night of close shaves. We listened to the German version of the raid and the announcer finished by saying that their defences had accounted for 49 British aircraft, while our own official figures were given as 48. We of our crew of course argued that the one difference must have been our aircraft which the gunners had wrongly claimed as a victim although, in fairness to them, in view of our behaviour over the target, it must have appeared a 'cert' for them. Although we laughed at such 'monstrous lies', we did breathe a sigh of relief when we thought of what might have been.

HOME FOR TEA *A white-tailed formation leader lands back at Waddington, home of 463 and 467 Aussie Squadrons, after a daylight sortie in the summer of 1944.*

From the spring of 1944, the 'softening up' for the invasion began with attacks on communications and oil, etc. With aerial superiority virtually complete, Bomber Command increasingly converted to daylight bombing.

Difficulty was often experienced with identification in the air and Nos. 1 and 5 Groups in particular painted fins and rudders to indicate the base, each base consisting of three stations.

Various combinations of stripes were also applied to wings and fuselage, the paint usually being a washable distemper.

THE HOME FIRE BURNING as a 576 Squadron Lanc comes in to land (top) at Fiskerton over FIDO towards the close of the war.

Not only did Bomber Command have to contend with enemy fighters and flak, the weather was a constant problem. Treacherous low-lying fog often greeted the tired crews on their return and, low on fuel, many kites crashed or had to be abandoned.

The answer was FIDO (Fog Investi-gation Dispersal Operation) albeit an expensive one. From the first operational use on the night of November 19/20, 1943, when four Halifaxes of 35 Squadron landed safely at Graveley, some 2,486 allied aircraft landed by it at the fifteen airfields thus equipped (1,200 at Woodbridge alone), at the expenditure of 100,000 tons of petrol.

MINIONS OF THE MOON Back from Berlin in the moonlit early hours, two Lancs (above) of 106 Squadron taxi back to their dispersals at Syerston in January 1943, using inboard engines only. The usual small clusters of ground crew await their crews' return no matter what the hour or weather.

This beautiful picture seems to epitomise more than any other the atmosphere of wartime operations by night.

Caterpillars Extraordinaire

'Blue' Rackley

The Caterpillar Club is a unique band of men and women whose lives have been saved with the aid of an Irving parachute. Records of the club contain several thousand reports of parachute descents and among them are to be found many incredible stories of courage, fortitude and amazing luck.

A Bomber Command crew which had its fair share of all three was that of F/O L. N. 'Blue' Rackley, a young red-headed Australian. They joined 630 Squadron at East Kirkby in mid-March 1944 and on their seventh trip had crash-landed on an airstrip in Corsica, after a tough trip to Munich in which they had lost their rear gunner. That Lanc had broken its back; but now, less than two months later, they were doing their ninth trip in their new BI, ME795 LE-G, a map of Corsica resplendent on the nose.

The Caterpillar Club files record the widely differing experiences of F/O Rackley and his Australian bomb aimer, P/O D. S. Morgan. Alas, their sixteenth trip – to attack the hydrogenisation plant at Wesseling in the Ruhr on June 21, 1944 – was fated to be their last together.

Soon after we crossed the Dutch coast we began to see aircraft exploding, so many in fact that I was almost convinced they were spoofs, until suddenly it was our turn. I had just brought the kite to a straight and level attitude after a banking search, when there was a terrific explosion aft, coupled with a muffled cry from one of my gunners.

We were thrown into a steep dive and it took all of 5,000 feet to recover. It was beyond my strength to pull back the control column and I had to call on the aid of Stan Jones, the flight engineer. Together we managed to pull out of the dive.

A Ju88 had attacked from beneath and broken away to port. Jack Jones, the mid-upper, scored some hits and the fighter was last seen on fire in the clouds.

Having righted the aircraft, it was immediately evident that the control surfaces were severely damaged. All aileron control was lost and I was unable to hold back the stick without assistance. She was answering very sloppily to the rudders and the situation looked grim.

The crew reported a large hole in the floor, just forward of the rear turret, but no other damage could be seen in the gloom. I decided to jettison the bombload and attempt to return to base. The engines were not damaged and the noise of four Merlins never sounded sweeter. The radio and intercom were serviceable so at least we had a chance.

Bit by bit we coaxed her through the turn, but it must have been the last straw for, soon after completing the turn, something appeared to snap and the rudder pedals sprang into the 'starboard rudder full on' position. She veered very slowly to starboard and I found that by placing both feet on the port pedal and exerting full pressure, I could bring the pedals to the neutral position and even get a little port rudder on. However, it was beyond my strength to keep this up, so Des Morgan, the bomb aimer, who by this time was up in the cockpit, took it in turns with the engineer to help me hold the stick back. One of them found some rope aboard. Just why it was there no one knew, but it was certainly welcome.

With the rudder pedals in the neutral position, a length of rope was lashed round the starboard pedal while the other end was secured to a part of the framework of the aircraft. This relieved the strain on my legs and kept us near enough to a straight course. What wander there was tended to be to starboard, and I was able to counteract this by exerting pressure with both legs on the port pedal from time to time.

We had no aileron control, but good fortune was with us and the kite did not drop a wing throughout the return trip. More rope was produced and the control column lashed in the neutral position. The bomb aimer stood by with an axe, ready to cut the rope should the need arise. We were now flying straight and level at about 10,000 feet, headed for England, under reasonable control, but with a long way to go.

Over the sea, 'Taffy' Davis, the rear gunner, was assisted from his turret up forward of the gaping hole in the floor. Lifting his chute from the clips on the side of the fuselage, he saw to his horror that it was badly damaged. We did not carry a spare so it was clear we had one helluva problem for there seemed a very slim chance of making England and landing the aircraft in its condition. I announced to the crew that we would have to bale out, and immediately the bomb aimer volunteered to take the rear gunner with him on his chute. Still more rope was produced and a scheme to tie the two men together was discussed. The plan was that as soon as we crossed the English coast, all the crew would leave the aircraft. With the engineer and myself on board, we thought we would stay with the kite, fly straight across England and bale out as she crossed the west coast, hoping she would continue for some distance before crashing into the sea.

It sounded a good plan, but as the journey progressed I realised it was an unlikely one. Gradually, what control I had began to deteriorate.

We crossed the coast somewhere near Ipswich. Immediately the bomb aimer and rear gunner, tied together, baled out through the forward hatch, followed closely by the mid-upper, wireless op and navigator.

Soon afterwards our wander to starboard became more pronounced. To make matters worse, some starboard bank came on, and since we had no aileron control the only method of correction was opposite rudder. However, I could not get enough on, or hold it long enough to be really effective, so it was evident that very soon the kite would be completely uncontrollable.

The original plan, to fly to the west coast before abandoning, was to prevent any loss of life or damage to property which may occur if the aircraft crashed on land. This was now out of the question, and with a doomed Lanc on our hands, it was time for the engineer and myself to leave.

The engineer dropped through the front escape hatch, followed very closely by myself. I went head first through the hatch in the approved manner, started to count as soon as I was clear, turned head-over-heels several times, sighting the wingtip lights of the Lanc at each turn, then at the count of five, I pulled the cord.

The chute opened and all the physical exhilaration of falling free in space ceased. I had lost a flying boot and my left foot was feeling very cold. So I tucked it inside the leg of my right boot for warmth.

Suddenly, I became aware of an aircraft approaching. The noise of engines became louder and louder, and when I saw it pass some distance overhead in a starboard turn I realised it was my Lanc! The engine tone diminished for a minute or so, but then increased once more; my kite was going round in circles, getting nearer the ground on each turn. This time she passed some distance beneath me, still in the starboard turn but the danger of a collision had passed. I heard the engines for some time; then suddenly an orange glow lit up the clouds below, followed by an almighty explosion. I could not help feeling I had lost a faithful friend.

Far below me I could see the tops of the cloud cover, and for some time I did not appear to be getting any closer to it; it appeared I was being carried upwards instead of downwards. In the darkness of early morning, it was difficult to tell.

Eventually I reached the clouds. The base must have been quite low, because no sooner had I passed through than I realised I was being dragged along at a terrific rate and became aware of the distinctive sound made by train wheels rattling beside my ear. I was being bumped about something awful, but it didn't seem to hurt. Neither was I aware of any fear. That came some days later! Looking back, it was a strange few seconds.

Then there is a blank. I remember finding myself beside a railway line. It was still dark and I had no idea where on earth I was. My second flying boot had disappeared, as had my watch. My chute was also gone. I found later that it had got caught up in the train, causing quite a stir on its arrival in London, when a search party was sent back along the line.

I think that while I was being dragged along by the train, the quick-release button of the chute must have been smashed, so that the harness straps were released, ripping the chute from me.

Dazed, I started to walk along the line. My head was bleeding, my shoulder was hurting and I could not move my right arm at all. After walking for some distance I heard a train approaching. When it came into view I could see it was travelling very slowly and was a goods train. Waiting until the engine was almost opposite me, I called to the crew for help. They answered and stopped the train.

The driver and fireman came down from the engine, followed by the guard shortly afterwards. I told them who I was and what had happened, but I think they had some doubt about my story. After some fast talking, the driver pulled the train along and I got into the guard's van. The guard sat outside on the platform and I suspect he thought I was a German and wasn't taking any chances with me.

The train stopped at a signal box to arrange for an ambulance to meet it at Luton and on arrival there, an ambulance and police escort took me to Luton and Dunstable Hospital.

Of the others in my crew, Taffy Davis, the rear gunner, was killed; but Des Morgan, the bomb aimer, landed safely, though badly shaken by his experience. When the chute opened he was unable to hold the gunner and he fell to the ground.

Ian Gow, the navigator, hit his arm against the tailwheel, fracturing his elbow. 'Curly' Carroll, the wireless op, arrived at a farmhouse with his parachute folded over his arm, but was threatened with a rifle by the occupant! He went on his way and found assistance elsewhere.

Stan Jones, the engineer, had an uneventful descent, but Jack Jones, the mid-upper, became entangled in the branches of a tree. In the dark he could not judge his distance from the ground, so decided to remain where he was until daylight. After a while he began to feel cold so kicked his legs to get warm. In doing so he stubbed his foot against a fence post. He was no more than two or three feet from the ground!

BRAKES ON – CUT ENGINES
Skippered by F/Sgt Clive Roantree, RAAF, 49 Squadron's D-Dog BIII, JB362 EA-D, is marshalled into her dispersal at Fiskerton, landing lights still piercing the night, after a trip to 'The Big City', November 18/19, 1943.

Being some 16 feet up, crews could see little of the immediate ground area when taxying, and to assist the pilot, the bomb aimer shines an Aldis lamp from the nose.

A picture taken during the opening rounds of the Battle of Berlin, which began in earnest on November 18/19, 1943, and ended with the 16th attack on March 24/25, 1944. Of Bomber Command's 9,111 sorties against Berlin, 7,256 were by Lancs.

FIRST BACK *All the joy of again being back on terra firma shows in this crew's faces as they gratefully tumble out at dispersal. Here at Waddington in January 1944, P/O Alec Riley, RAAF, and his 467 Squadron crew are first back from Berlin, unshaven dishevelled but happy. After eight hours in a Lanc, ears would be ringing from the noise of the engines for a long time afterwards, making sleep difficult. It would be some time before the feet and legs became accustomed to firm ground again, with no movement or vibration.*

BACK FOR BREAKFAST *Despite a tiring nine-hour trip to Genoa in the winter of 1942, a group of 106 Squadron aircrew can still manage a smile for the cameraman at Syerston in the early morning light.*

The Lanc BI, R5573 *named* Admiral – Foo-Banc V, *is one of several specially fitted with bulged bomb doors for the carriage of 8,000lb bombs. The doors, made of wood with rubber hinges, opened by the sheer weight of the bomb dropping on them. Devised at Group level, their shape gave rise to the nickname 'pot belly'.*

ALL SMILES *The elation of this 467 Squadron Aussie crew is obvious as they pile aboard the crew truck at Bottesford in the early morning after the night's operation. Their object now is to get interrogation over as quickly as possible, breakfast on bacon and eggs, then catch up on some sleep.*

AFTER THE RAID

INTERROGATION *The raid is over and the crews – not really in the mood for it – are questioned painstakingly by the Intelligence Officer. "What was the flak like? Any fighters? How many kites did you see go down?"*

This is the scene at Bardney in the early hours of January 6, 1944, as F/Lt Paddy Ervine and his 9 Squadron crew discuss the attack on Stettin, fortified by mugs of tea, well laced with rum.

BEER ALL ROUND *as W/Cdr 'Tubby' Baker, CO of 635 Squadron, Downham Market, returns from his 100th trip (all done on Wimpeys, Stirlings and Lancs), a 'daylight' to Wuppertal, March 13, 1945.*

If you were lucky enough to survive one tour you could be called for a second after a period of 'rest' at a training unit as an instructor, but the chances of completing it were slim indeed.

After two tours you could not be called back; but such was the spirit that some went on and on.

BRINGING BACK THE EMPTIES
Spent cartridge cases indicate a busy night. In general there were few head-on attacks by fighters and normally the only time the bomb aimer would be called upon as a gunner was during daylight attacks by fighters, or on those rare occasions when some strafing of trains was undertaken at low level.

LANCS AT REST 1 *The day's work is done and all is quiet. 149 Squadron's Lancs at rest at Methwold as dusk approaches on a late summer's evening in 1944.*

CALL SIGN FG6		97 SQUADRON			DATE 30/31 /9_

M.S.I	AIRCRAFT (Letter / No.)	CREW	TAKE OFF (Est / Actual)	EST. TIME OVER TARGET	RETURN (Est / Actual)	NOTES
1×4000 8SBCs OF 4LBS	V / R5487	W/O Collier, F/S Turner, F/O Hooey, Sgt Brummitt, F/O Irould, Sgt Martin, F/S Jones	0001 / 0003		0400 / 0401	CAMERA
1×4000 8SBCs OF 4LBS	M / R5502	Flt Hallows, F/S Louch, F/O Friend, Sgt Jones L, F/O Cutting, Sgt Bromfield, Sgt Goacher	/ 0007		/ 0345	
1×4000 8SBCs OF 4LBS	G / R5614	F/S Berridge, Sgt Fleming, F/O Long, Sgt Hellyer, Sgt Connely, Sgt Buxton, Sgt McPhee	/ 0034		/ 0519	CAMERA
1×4000 8SBCs OF 4LBS	H / R5538	Plt Miller, Sgt Robertson, F/S Cullinane, Sgt Smith L, Sgt Grossmith, Sgt Nickerson, F/S Westgate	/ 0009		/ 0455	
1×4000 8SBCs OF 4LBS	I / L7577	Plt Coton, Sgt Newell, Sgt Kruger, Sgt Martin P, F/O Boddington, Robinson, Sgt McMahon	/ 0014		/ 0547	CAMERA
1×4000 8SBCs OF 4LBS	W / R5559	F/O Deverill, Sgt Irons, Sgt Cooper, Sgt Devine, F/O Butler, Sgt Benbow, Sgt Keane	/ 0011		/ 0339	CAMERA
1×4000 8SBCs OF 4LBS	Z / R5497	F/O Hughes, F/O Crerar, Sgt Lawton, Sgt Harris, Sgt Walker, Sgt Mercer, Sgt Overton	/ 0016		/ 0529	CAMERA
1×4000 8SBCs OF 4LBS	J / R5558	Sgt McMurchy, F/O Richardson, Sgt Morgan, Sgt Girvin, F/O Williams, Sgt Hesdon, Sgt Barraclough				CANCELLED REAR WHEEL BROKE
1×4000 8SBCs OF 4LBS	A / R5571	Sgt Davies, Sgt Goodwin, F/O Keough, Smith E, Sgt McMechan, Sgt Coone, Sgt Goddard	/ 0030		/ 0513	CAMERA
1×4000 8SBCs OF 4LBS	U / R5496	F/O Adams, Sgt Stafford, F/S Falls, Sgt Dawson, Sgt Creeth, F/O Goldie, Sgt Linnett	/ 0037		/ 0539	CAMERA
1×4000 8SBCs OF 4LBS	X / R5607	F/S Fletcher, Sgt Wilkinson, F/O McKenna, Sgt Garland, F/O Blair, P/O K Hackett, F/O Bale	/ 0039		/ 0544	CAMERA
1×4000 8SBCs OF 4LBS	F / R5572	F/O Rodley, Sgt Merralls, P/O Colquhoun, Sgt Cummings, F/O Bennett, Sgt Ratcliffe, Sgt Crisp	/ 0031		/ 0416	
1×4000 8SBCs OF 4LBS	S / R5609	F/O Hartley, Sgt Gross, F/O Briant, Sgt Mayland, W/O Canham, Sgt Suckling, F/O Legge	/ 0044		/ 0526	
1×4000 8SBCs OF 4LBS	C / R5512	Flt Blakeman, Sgt Nicholl, F/O Blease, Sgt Allen, F/O Shrybman, F/O Trueman, F/O McKenzie	/ 0055		/ 0504	
1×4000 8SBCs OF 4LBS	P / R5552	W/O Harrison, Sgt Preston, Sgt Crouch, Sgt Farara, Sgt Platten, Sgt Townley, F/O Oates	/ 0042		/ 0541	
1×4000 8SBCs OF 4LBS	R / R5612	F/S Kelleher, F/O Baines, Sgt Griffiths, Sgt Bunt, Sgt Cook, Sgt Guy, Sgt Desmond	/ 0046		/ 0302	RETURNED EARLY ENGINE TROUBLE

DUTY INTELLIGENCE OFFICER – CONINGSBY   P/O STENNING   DUTY INTELLIGENCE OFFICER   F/O BURNABY

ALL BACK SAFELY *The 97 Squadron operations board at Woodhall Spa after the historic 1,000-Bomber Raid on Cologne, May 30/31, 1942 – Operation Millennium. Having only recently been introduced into squadron service, and still in short supply, Lancasters represented only 6.5 per cent of the total force of 1,047 aircraft dispatched, but only one of the 67 failed to return. A Lanc from 61 Squadron's Conversion Flight had the dubious distinction of being the last aircraft over the target. Because of their greater speed, the Lancs took off much later than other types used on the raid.*

A cool welcome

Ken Lane

At take-off conditions could be perfect, yet only a few hours later the bombers could run into vicious storms, with towering cumulo-nimbus clouds tossing them around like straws in the wind.

A cold front could cause ice to build up, often freezing control surfaces, while gale force winds could drive the stream many miles off track.

On the night of March 30/31, 1944, Bomber Command encountered phenomenal weather conditions and suffered as a result its worst single setback of the whole war. Moreover, the target, Nuremberg, was only slightly damaged.

Conditions over the North Sea made it impossible to arrange a large-scale diversion, while the difficulty of predicting changeable March winds led to serious errors in navigation. The high cloud – expected to give concealment – dispersed, leaving the aircraft silhouetted against the lower clouds. Added to this, the aircraft left vapour trails in the intensely cold but clear atmosphere, each taking on a phosphorescent glow in the light of a half moon.

The Luftwaffe correctly deduced the direction of approach from H2S bearings. 'Bomber' Harris and his staff had a shrewd idea of the dangers of using H2S, but they had little choice. On this night some 200 night fighters lay in wait and wreaked fearful havoc. The final toll was to be 95 Lancasters and Halifaxes, besides a further 11 written off after their return.

Thick cloud covered the target and, with the Path Finder Force late, the main force had to mill around, increasing the risk of collision. Impatient crews began to drop their loads anywhere. Even when the markers did go down, 47 minutes late, they could not be seen through the clouds.

W/O Ken Lane and crew of 83 Pathfinder Squadron missed the fighters, but ran into atrocious weather on their return to England. Incredibly, their Lanc BIII, ND333 OL-F, stayed in the air, when by all the laws of aerodynamics she should have crashed.

Some people are able to remember incidents or dates without difficulty, but with me it has to be something really outstanding to maintain a lasting impression in my mind.

The night of March 30, 1944, when I piloted a Lancaster to Nuremberg is a night I cannot forget because my memory is reinforced by three basic points. First, this was the night of the big wind. Second, it was the night when the Lancaster showed qualities which endeared her to all who flew in her. Third, the question is posed, Was this the biggest air defeat of the war?

When Nuremberg was discussed at briefing, there were no exclamations or subdued murmurs such as usually arose when Berlin was mentioned. Not that any target was easy, but Nuremberg did not appear to be worthy of undue comment, and naturally no one could be aware of events to follow.

Wind speed and direction at a given height was of paramount navigational importance to aircraft of the main force, but perhaps for the Pathfinders it was of lesser importance, as special equipment was carried which made it reasonably easy for navigators to find new winds. Using these new winds, appropriate corrections were made and the result was amazing accuracy in navigation which enabled aircraft to be over a given spot at the exact time planned.

I was privileged to be a Pathfinder in 83 Squadron, and although briefing had given us 80-knot winds, we found when proceeding over the enemy coast at 22,000 feet that the wind was now 120–130 knots! Much of the ground was hidden under heavy cloud, making it almost impossible to obtain a 'fix', and as we made the necessary course adjustment, I sympathised with aircraft of the main force who would certainly be experiencing more difficulty.

Flying in darkness can be very lonely, with little or no conversation between crew members, and it was sometimes quite a relief to be almost turned over by the slipstream of an unseen aircraft or to see flames from four belching exhausts spitting at you through the gloom. At least you knew that another aircraft was in front and going in the same direction. However, even this reassurance was lacking on this loneliest of all nights when there was nothing to be seen apart from the occasional glow in the distance. This probably resulted from aircraft being blown off course and drifting over heavily defended areas. Routes were planned with great care to avoid danger spots, and to wander off made for a rough flight.

We were still above broken cloud over the target, where our function was to drop four flares visually to build up those dropped earlier by other Pathfinders, and to add for good measure 8,000lb of high-explosive bombs. This we did with only slight interference from flak, which was rather scattered, and then came the welcome time to turn for home.

The journey was a repetition of the outward flight, without incident of note, but the real problem was to come when we arrived over our base at Wyton. Weather conditions around this part were atrocious with a snowstorm giving nil visibility. All other aircraft had been diverted, but because of a radio fault we were not informed, and now we were in the unenviable position of having to land without assistance from the ground.

Several attempts to approach were made, but each time the runway was lost, and after nearly hitting the water tower, I decided to use Standard Beam Approach procedure which in those days was the popular aid to a blind landing. Picking up the beam, I made my circuit and approach, gradually losing height at the appropriate rate of descent. When only a few seconds from touch-down, I suddenly saw the runway contact lights and, as the colour was red, I realised that I was too far along the runway for a landing. I commenced to carry out my overshoot drill, but when I pushed on the throttles nothing happened; the linkage was probably frozen. As I strained harder, so my seat catch could not stand the backward pressure and, jumping from its locked position, the seat dropped to its lowest point, leaving my head about a foot below vision level. Airspeed literally dropped off the clock, and although well below stalling speed, the amazing Lanc remained airborne. The more I think about this, the more fantastic it appears when one considers a heavy four-engined bomber still flying at little over 65 knots.

As I fought to control the aircraft, I also managed to raise my seat to a higher level, and the return of vision brought full realisation of the extent of the danger. We skimmed across fields and hedgerows which even at this low altitude were not very distinct, but the grim certainty was that we would hit something solid before much longer. Suddenly the throttle levers gave and the engines roared into full life, bringing at least some hope of survival. Even so, height was needed to recover from a near-stall, and we didn't have this luxury; but the wonderful Lanc responded to every touch and gradually reached a safe speed, making it possible for us to climb to comparative safety.

Fuel was running low, but after completing another circuit and approach, a landing was achieved. Conditions on the ground were certainly grim, and the Aerodrome Control Pilot in his caravan claimed later that he had not seen an aircraft actually land, although he had heard some frightening noises.

There was no sign of life on the station, and the duty officer had to be roused to de-brief us, much to his disgust. For us it was a case of 'all's well that ends well', but on the radio next morning we heard the sombre news that 95 aircraft were missing. Others would probably have run out of fuel and crash-landed, but I never heard the final toll.

What a night this had been, with very few aircraft actually reaching the target; but the question as to whether this was Bomber Command's costliest mission remains unanswered.

For me this was the night when the Lancaster bomber performed the impossible.

LANCS AT REST 2 *460 Squadron Binbrook, spring 1944. In the background is the pre-war type of hangar, still in use at Binbrook today.*

BATTLE DAMAGE

FRIENDS OR FOES *Being hit by bombs or incendiaries from a kite above was a constant threat. At night the dangers were not so obvious to the crews, but on the mass day-light raids of 1944 and 1945 it was often difficult to find a safe gap over the target.*

The rear turret of this PFF Lanc was completely sheared off by a falling bomb, leaving the ammunition belts and hydraulic feed pipes hanging. The gunner disappeared with his turret.

Above is 156 Squadron BIII, ND340 GT-S, with a gaping hole left by a 'friendly' bomb over Fort D'Enghos petrol dump August 9, 1944. Mercifully, the bomb did not go off and F/Lt J. A. Wilson and crew all got back safely.

"95 OF OUR AIRCRAFT ARE MISSING . . ." *were the terse words of the communique after the disastrous raid on Nuremberg on the night of March 30/31, 1944. However, the figure did not include the many aircraft wrecked or so badly damaged that they either never flew again or were sent for a rebuild.*

Below is the battered interior of the rear fuselage of a 9 Squadron Lanc BI, DV395 WS-V, caught by fighters from underneath (a favourite attacking position), killing the mid-upper gunner: the dark stains on the floor, doorstep and Elsan tell their own grim story. By a cool-headed piece of flying, F/O Harry Forrest nursed his mount home.

Bomber Command had come a long way since the pioneering days of 1940/1, but even with the sophisticated equipment and techniques available in 1944, things could still go wrong. On this occasion, not only did the Luftwaffe guess the target correctly, but the 'met' boobed: instead of the forecast cloud cover, there was bright moonlight, 150 mph tailwinds and severe icing.

THE FIGHTER MENACE *Steel rods show the angle of penetration from a night fighter's shells in the port wing of this Lanc BIII, ND356/G from 100 Squadron, Waltham.*

Attacked over Stuttgart March 15/16, 1944, S/Ldr Hugh Grant-Dalton and crew got away by superb teamwork and full use of the 'corkscrew'.

HOME HAZARD *This 97 (Straits Settlements) Squadron Lanc, BIII, ND495, OF-M, returned safely from a night op in August 1944, but on turning off the peri-track at Coningsby, was struck by another taxying Lancaster with disastrous results. Bad though the damage appears, she had returned to ops within a month as OF-N, complete with new tail section. Although the accident occurred at night, the tail markings distinguish this aircraft as a daylight formation leader.*

GROUND ATTACK *Not all Lancs were lost by aerial combats. These two were photographed after a surprise 'last ditch' attack by enemy fighters on Ursel (Belgium) where the Lancs had made emergency landings, taking advantage of airfields captured by the Allies. The foam seems to be taking effect on this kite* (left) *but there is no hope for the other one* (below left).

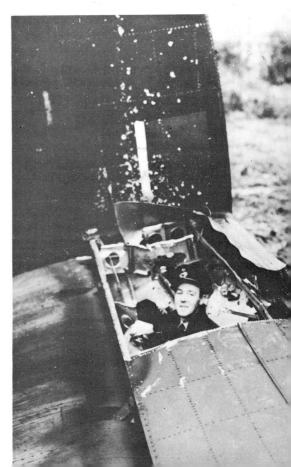

ONE WAY OF LOOKING AT IT
F/Lt Ron Gill of 635 Squadron finishes his second tour with a bang! Here at Downham Market he ruefully examines the flak-damaged tailplane of his Lanc BIII, ND735 F2-L, after returning from a night attack on Dusseldorf on November 2/3, 1944. The starboard aileron was also hit and immoveable and it was a near-miracle the Lanc made base at all.

PRANGS

CRASH-LANDED *For getting this badly shot-up Lanc home in spite of severe injuries to himself and his crew, F/Lt Bill Reid won the VC. The effects of two night-fighter attacks can be clearly seen. The skipper's own account tells only too graphically how terror could strike:*

"3/11/43 BIII, LM360 QR-O 'self and crew Op. No. 10' Dusseldorf. 5h 30m (night) Attacked by Me110 at Dutch Coast. R/G was unable to open fire due to a heating failure, thus his hands were frozen. The I/C was u/s so he was also unable to give avoiding action orders or warning. By supreme effort he did open fire after a brief delay, but not before the N/F had raked us from stem to stern. However, the N/F was driven off. By now the rear turret was almost useless, the compass was u/s, the elevator trim tabs were u/s and the kite kept wallowing. The windscreen was shattered and I was wounded in the head, shoulders and hands. We continued on track but were suddenly attacked by a Fw190 which riddled us all over on two passes. The Nav. was killed instantly and the W/Op badly wounded. The R/G tried hard to hit the fighter but only one gun would function and the turret packed up altogether. The M/U turret was hit, stopped and the oxygen system put u/s. I was hit too and started losing blood fast. The F/E gave me oxygen from the portable supply. The F/E was himself injured.

"We carried on and reached the target bang on track. Had memorised the course luckily. We left the target and set course by the Pole star and moon. I was growing weak now from loss of blood and the oxygen supply was no more. The cold air coming in from the shattered cockpit was freezing. The F/E and B/A between them flew the kite back. On sighting land they looked for the first airfield visible, revived me and we came in to land at what turned out to be Shipdham, a Yank liberator base. There was some ground mist and I could not see the runway lights. Blood kept getting into my eyes and I was almost fainting. The F/E and B/A were both holding myself and the column with all their might. One leg of the undercart collapsed but there was no fire."

ROUGH TRIP *This was how BIII, PB114 GT-N, finished a raid on Hamburg on July 28/29, 1944. It was the last op of the skipper's third tour (S/Ldr H. F. Slade, RAAF) and the account which follows shows just how lucky he and his crew were to get away with it:*

The kite was hit by flak before the run-in to the target. After the bombs had been released she went into a slow spiral dive, completely out of control. The crew stood by ready to bale out but control was regained. With the aid of the nav and flight engineer, the pilot manhandled the stricken kite out of the target area, but with only 10 per cent of aileron control. They had an anxious time over the coastal gun belt because no evading action could be taken for fear of losing control. By intelligent use of petrol from the port tanks only, a better balance was achieved and this eased the flying condition. Once over the North Sea they headed for Woodbridge and though all engines were undamaged height was slowly being lost all the way. Any momentary loss of power or relaxation in the grim struggle with the controls would have sent them into the sea. Woodbridge was reached at an altitude of only 1,500 ft and a successful emergency wheels-up landing made at 03.15 hrs. All the crew were unharmed but the damage was extensive, the port outer engine being completely wrecked.

RECOVERY *Very bent, and with engine air intakes filled with earth, an early Lanc, R5845 of 1660 Conversion Unit, Swinderby, is lifted ready for the recovery trolley by a crew of 58 MU.*

Looking rather sorry for itself, the nose is taken away on a 'Queen Mary' for salvage of parts and eventual scrap, the other sections following behind. The scene is somewhat reminiscent of a funeral procession. The camouflage is an unusual pattern for a Lanc, being a leftover from Manchester days.

JUST GOOD FRIENDS *When the movable meets the immovable, the result of a Lanc travelling at over 100 mph colliding with a stationary Fortress.*

On the night of March 24/25, 1944, the 16th and last major attack in the Battle of Berlin – F/Sgt Fred Brownings and crew of 103 Squadron, on their fifth operation, were severely mauled by a Fw190 in a running fight. All turrets were put out of action and the rear gunner killed. With the flaps shot away, tanks holed, both rudders shattered, most of the cockpit instruments smashed, inter-com u/s, the Lanc BIII, ND572

THE MORNING AFTER *In the early light of a cold winter's morning, November 28, 1943, Mr T. C. Langton, Avro's assistant repair manager surveys this frost-covered Lanc BIII, JB354 PH-O, of 12 Squadron. Returning to Wickenby damaged after the night's raid on Berlin, P/O R. S. Yell, RAAF, had swung on landing; the port undercarriage leg was ripped off and the kite declared a write-off.*

PM-M, was extremely difficult to hold. To make matters worse, they were shot up by flak on the way home.

With no chance of making their home base of Elsham Wolds, the wireless operator got a fix on Dunsfold. By superb flying, the skipper brought her in but, without any brakes, she swung off the runway and suddenly hit something extremely solid in the

early morning gloom.

Dazed but miraculously unhurt, the crew were astonished to see that they had crashed into a parked B-17G Fortress of the USAAF. Both were a sorry sight and had to be written off. Closer inspection revealed a six-foot hole in the port wing and hundreds of flak holes.

DITCHING WITH A DIFFER-ENCE *Some crews came through a tour with little or no trouble while others met nothing but trouble, F/O Peter Todd and crew of 61 Squadron survived this prang without injury but were not so lucky the second time, ending up in the Channel after their 16th trip, to Berlin on March 24/25, 1944, being picked up by a German launch and spending the remainder of the war 'in the bag'.*

On their way to Mannheim, on the night of September 5/6, 1943 – only their second operation – their BIII, DV232 QR-K, lost an engine when the port outer caught fire. The Graviner had some effect and, with the prop feathered, they pressed on, bombed, and headed for home.

Coming in to land at Syerston, with Todd desperately trying to keep the approach at 120 mph she suddenly stalled to port, narrowly missing some station buildings. Staggering over the countryside at zero feet, she finally did a steep turn and literally 'belly-flopped' into the Trent half a mile north of East Stoke, near Newark.

H/9 F/O KEELEY. TALAGI AREA.

DOWN IN RUSSIA *While some Lancs amassed an impressive number of sorties, others achieved but one or two. F/O Les Keeley's Lanc BI, NF938 WS-H, lies wrecked in a bog in the Talagi area, ten miles from Yagodnik near Archangel in Russia, having done just one op.*

One of the force making up Operation Paravane, the destruction of the Tirpitz once and for all, Keeley and his 9 Squadron crew failed to locate Yagodnik airfield in the early hours of September 12, 1944, due to low cloud.

Having made an 11-hour flight from Lossiemouth, petrol was rapidly running out and after five runs and several square searches, a forced landing became inevitable. After jettisoning the load of 'Johnny Walker' bombs in a river, the crew put down in open marshland (left). No one was injured.

Two other kites from No. 9 and two from No. 617 Squadron were wrecked in similar fashion, and though salvage was not possible, much equipment was recovered.

As is well known, the attack on September 15 by the Russian-based force failed to sink the ship but she was badly damaged and her fate finally sealed.

H/9 F/Lt CAMSELL. BELOMORSK.

F/Lt George Camsell's BI, PD211 WS-M, also of 9 Squadron (left), after the undercarriage had collapsed on the rough wooden planking airstrip of Belomorsk.

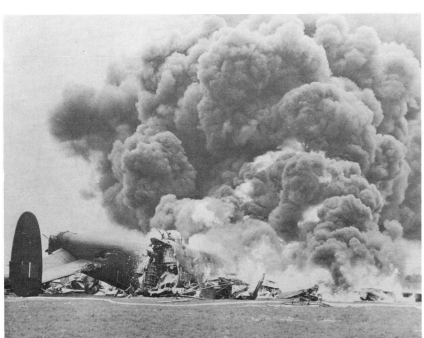

BURN UP *Some crews hit trouble even before they reached a squadron. F/Sgt J. P. Paddison and crew of 1668 CU Bottesford, had an engine fire on a cross-country training flight but managed to force-land their BIII, JB228, at Fiskerton, where it burns fiercely on March 10, 1945.*

THE FAMOUS FALLEN *The most-photographed Lanc of the war comes to grief; Lanc BI, R5689 VN-N, of 50 Squadron, lies broken in a field at Thurlby (above right). Borrowed by Sgt E. J. Morley and crew for a 'gardening' sortie on September 18/19, 1942, both port engines failed on the approach due to a mechanical fault.*

Though Lancasters had been operating since March 1942, little information had been released to the public except for news of the remarkable low-level daylight op to Augsburg on April 17. On August 28 of that year the free world's press descended on 50 Squadron at Swinderby. S/Ldr Hughie Everitt, a Flight Commander on his second tour,

gave a vivid demonstration of the aircraft's performance and handling qualities in his beloved 'N-Nan' (above left).

For the remainder of the war photos of her appeared in books, periodicals and advertisements and even the Germans used reproductions on propaganda leaflets.

QUEEN ELIZABETH, *Lanc BI R5548 OF-A, ended her days at Woodhall Spa on December 28, 1942, when her own photoflashes went off inside the fuselage.*

Autographed by HM Queen Elizabeth (now the Queen Mother) on the production line at Yeadon on March 20, 1942, she went to 97 (Straits

Settlements) Squadron and is seen (below left) in her prime with S/Ldr 'Darky' Hallows driving, and who did most of his tour in her.

Irony of fate – he salvaged the nose panel only to have it stolen a year or so later when serving as Chief Instructor at Winthorpe Conversion Unit, and still awaits its return!

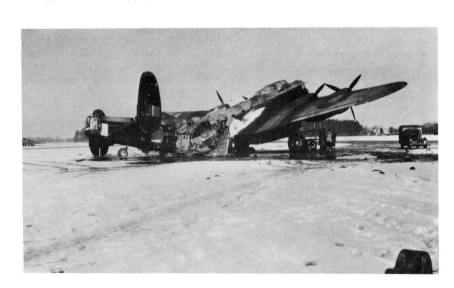

UNDER REPAIR

REPAIR SHOP *Damaged aircraft and those lucky enough to survive 500 hours flying were taken for repair or overhaul to a depot such as the LMS railway workshops at Derby, or one of Avro's own repair works, at Bracebridge Heath or Langar. The sections would be divided into nose (D1), mainplane (D2 and F1), fuselage (D3), and tail (D4), each being taken into a different shop. After overhaul, the sections would be reassembled on a 'first off the line' basis, meaning that*

rarely would the same four sections be married up again. Only the nose section would normally keep its original identity, particularly if it bore an emblem. These scenes at Langar in 1943 show (below) 'D1' nose sections being refurbished and (foot of page) the final re-assembly shop. The leading edge of the Lanc in the foreground is lifted to reveal a mass of pipes and wiring. On the inside of the raised panel are the cable cutters. If a balloon cable were hit it should slide along the leading edge

surface intil it became channelled into a 'V' shaped hole. The small detonator would then explode and fire across two hard steel chisels to cut right through the cable – whether the device ever worked in practice is not known. Also in the leading edge is the cabin air intake, and on the side of the cockpit, just below the camouflage line, is the drift sight. The cockpit frame-work is covered in a sealing tape which was painted 'dark earth' before being trimmed.

TEST PILOT *The resident Langar test pilot, S/Ldr Peter J. Field-Richards, signs the Form 700 watched by his Flight Test Observer, Bob Browne. Until the former's permanent attachment, test flights were carried out for Avro by pilots of No. 207 Squadron based at the same airfield. From the time Langar accepted its first Lancaster in September 1942 to the last one in July 1954, 322 were refurbished there.*

PREPARING FOR FLIGHT TEST *In late winter afternoon sunshine at Langar, November 1943, BI, ED430 is made ready after overhaul on a wet, partially completed dispersal. Parts of the aircraft round the tail and fins are still to be repainted.*

TAKE 'EM AWAY *The camera angle emphasises the size of the Lanc – big by any standards – as Capt H. A. ('Sam') Brown, an Avro test pilot, gives the thumbs-up to the ground crew before taxying an early machine for a test flight. She is finished in the original 'lamp black' extra-matt, which did not weather well, became powdery and rubbed off easily.*

It was superseded by a smoother paint with a slight sheen. The black finish applied to Lancs became progressively more glossy towards the end of the war, and some Canadian machines were given quite a high gloss final coat. On the starboard chock is Jack Denly.

INSIGNIA

The pawnbroker's sign was a popular feature on many a 'U-Uncle'. Above is BIII, ED480 WS-U of 9 Squadron at Waddington in February 1943, the Lanc in which F/Lt Bill Meyer and crew did a tour

The female form was without doubt the most popular adornment and here is a splendid example on a BX, KB747 NA-X Madam X, of 428 'Ghost' Squadron, RCAF, Middleton St George, in 1945. The bomb symbol presentation is somewhat unusual.

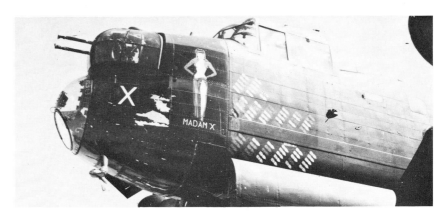

Not all female embellishments were flamboyant and here is one with a difference. F/O Peter Thompson and crew of 12 Squadron, Wickenby, chose Queen of the Chase for their BI, ME788 PH-Q, summer 1944.

A saintly lady is how BIII, PB532 HW-S² of 100 Squadron appeared to her crew. The name stems from the South American origins of her pilot, F/Lt O. Lloyd-Davies, and the style of the bomb symbols suggests there was a musician in the crew. The photograph was taken at Elsham Wolds in April 1945.

Some crews preferred a name instead of insignia and here is a particularly apt one, for aircrews liked their ale !

S/Ldr Dave Robb, RCAF, and his 100 Squadron crew drew many an admiring glance in the air with their BI, PA177 HW-J², Jug & Bottle. The photo was taken after the Squadron had moved from Waltham, its base since December 1942, to join 103 at Elsham Wolds in April 1945.

At Linton-on-Ouse in April 1944, a crewman pauses while painting on the insignia devised for a BII, LL725 EQ-Z of 408 'Goose' Squadron RCAF, and already credited with two confirmed fighters. Her usual skipper at this time was F/O E. M. C. Franklin, RCAF.

Many a Disney character emblazoned a kite but rarely more than a single figure on any one Lanc. Here are no less than seven on a BIII, PB480 TC-G² of 170 Squadron, Hemswell, in March 1945, on which F/Lt Bob Chandler and crew did a tour.

Most insignia were painted on the actual metal but some were done on canvas first and then stuck on; the artist in this example was the crew's wireless op, Sgt Ron Woodin.

The Daily Mirror's 'Jane' graced a number of kites and BIII, JB138 QR-J, Just Jane, of 61 Squadron went on to join the elite band of 100-op veterans. Between August 1943 and April 1945 she completed 123 sorties.

With suitable blowsy woman of doubtful virtue is Honky Tonk, *BIII*, PB229 *LQ-H* of 405 'Vancouver' Squadron, RCAF, Gransden Lodge, the mount of F/Lt Lance Burnand, RCAF, and crew for part of their tour in the autumn of 1944.

405 was No. 6 (Canadian) Group's contribution to Path Finder Force.

Often insignia had no apparent link with the aircraft. S/Ldr Peter Birch (here seen in the cockpit), a Flight Commander with 50 Squadron at Skellingthorpe in the spring of 1943, constantly whistled and hummed the tune The Donkey Serenade, so his crew had a donkey painted on their Lanc *BIII*, ED828 *VN-S*.

'Old Nick', the devil, was chosen by F/O Ray Hattam, RAAF, and crew of 463 Australian Squadron, Waddington, summer 1944. Each op is denoted by a pronged fork.

A *BI*, LM130 *JO-N*, she was one of several of 463's kites adapted to carry cameramen from the RAF's Film Unit. Apart from normal main force operations, they accompanied other squadrons on special raids, such as the Tirpitz attacks.

A caricature of himself featured on all kites flown by W/Cdr Campbell Hopcroft, CO of 57 Squadron at Scampton. This one (below) is his

third, Frederick III, *BIII*, ED989 *DX-F*, in May 1943. Henceforth he became known as 'Freddy' Hopcroft.

For their emblem S/Ldr Don Rogers, RCAF, and crew of 433 'Porcupine' Squadron, RCAF, had a very young female indeed. The crew's flight engineer Ron Broome proudly poses for a snapshot at Skipton-on-Swale, April 1945 in the cockpit of Little Lulu Mk II, *BI*, NG441 *BM-L*. Note the novel way each sortie is recorded. The crew's first Little Lulu was a Halifax, with which the Squadron was equipped until February 1945.

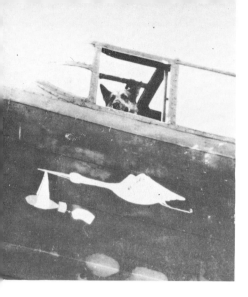

That well-known symbol of delivery, the stork, was chosen by F/O 'Tony' Davies and crew for their 7 Squadron Lanc BIII, EE129 MG-Y at Oakington, autumn 1943.

No. 7 was 3 Group's contribution to PFF.

Insignia combined with the call letter was the novel idea on BIII, ED539 PO-V, flown by P/O Bill Manifold, RAAF, and crew of 467 Squadron, Bottesford, in the summer of 1943.

A kookaburra dangles the head of Hitler from its beak. Crew decorations appear at the end of the bomb symbols.

Though the nose was the usual place, sometimes other parts came in for treatment. Below is Ropey, a veteran BX, KB772 VR-R, of 419 'Moose' Squadron RCAF, complete with shark's teeth and eyes on all four engine nacelles. Perhaps the skipper had flown Mustangs!

Crew nicknames appear under crew positions, a not uncommon feature.

Air Commodore A. Hesketh, Commander of 53 Base (Bardney, Skellingthorpe and Waddington), watches as the score is chalked on an 8,000lb bomb at Waddington to mark the 100th operation by 467's BI, R5868 PO-S, S-Sugar.

P/O T. N. Scholefield, RAAF, and crew took the old lady on her 100th trip, to Bourg Leopold on the night of May 11/12, 1944, and she went on to reach 137 before retirement.

Mistakenly thought to be Bomber Command's top-scoring 'heavy', and selected for preservation, she exists to this day and stood until recently at the gates of RAF Scampton, from where she first flew in June 1942 with 83 Squadron. She has now been removed to the RAF Museum.

100 NOT OUT

THE 100 OP LANCS There has always been – and, we suppose, always will be – controversy over how many aircraft actually completed 100 operational sorties; and also, whether certain aircraft reputed to have done 100 or more did, in fact, achieve the number of sorties represented on their noses by bomb symbols. Who is one to believe? The ground crews who so faithfully stencilled on another bomb the morning after each op? Or the clerk whose mundane job it was to compile the Operational Record Books? In some cases perhaps we shall never know the true answer however much research is undertaken. For example, there is now some doubt as to whether R5868, 'S-Sugar' did the 137 trips which her bomb motifs would suggest when she was finally withdrawn from service. The ORBs suggest she did only 121 ops, it being possible that the other 16 were added during Operations 'Exodus' and 'Dodge'. Or was she, perhaps, loaned to another squadron for a spell, and recorded in that

unit's ORBs as merely 'S' with no confirmatory serial number?

On some ops the trip would be cut short by recall, battle damage, mechanical trouble, crew illness, etc. At what stage was it counted as an op? Did the aircraft have to cross the enemy coast, or did the hours flown determine the answer? Perhaps the ground crew had their own interpretation of an op completed, which may have differed to that of the ops clerk. Instances have been noted in the ORBs where the clerk has, through habit, continued to quote an aircraft's serial against a code letter for some time after that particular machine is known to have been lost, withdrawn for overhaul, or transferred to another squadron. It could sometimes take several days for changes to be advised due to pressure of war, illness, etc. So, despite a long and exhaustive study of squadron records, it appears likely that some uncertainty will always surround odd aircraft. Unfortunately, aircrew log books, once again, usually compiled

somewhat unwillingly under pressure, contain inaccuracies and do not always provide reliable cross-references.

Whatever the facts and figures may show, let it be said that to achieve something like 1,000 hours of operational flying over an 18-month to two-year period, a Lanc had to possess certain qualities, including luck, durability, good crews (both air and ground), and – above all – a phenomenal standard of mechanical reliability. Apart from the two weeks or so it took to do 500 and 1,000 hour overhauls, a Lanc would rarely see the inside of a hangar. She would be required to stand outside on the most exposed of dispersals throughout most of her life in all weathers.

So far, 28 Lancasters have been traced as having completed the magic 100; other centenarians may turn up in the course of time. In the pages which follow, we show a selection of 100-op kites, some well known, others hitherto unknown.

Mickey the Moocher, *BIII*, EE176 *QR-M of 61 Squadron, Skellingthorpe, snapped in 1944 after 83 ops. She went on to complete 115 before retiring to become a ground instructional machine; at least, 115 was the number of bomb symbols on the nose, though official records show her as having done 128 ops.*

Unofficially adopted by the famous whisky firm, 9 Squadron's BI, W4964 WS-J, Johnny Walker *began operations in April 1943 and completed her century on September 15, 1944, dropping a 12,000lb tallboy on the Tirpitz in Alten Fjord, Norway.*

On their return to Bardney, F/Lt Doug. Melrose and his crew were presented with a crate of whisky.

After completing 106 trips she was pensioned off, became a ground instructional airframe and survived until scrapped in 1949.

Apart from numerous crew decorations, other symbols adorning the nose include wound stripes, and a searchlight.

Another Lanc whose century was achieved by food drops, represented by tins of spam instead of bomb symbols on the nose, is BIII, PB150 CF-V of 625 Squadron, Scampton.

Lanc BI, LM227 UL-I, I-Item, *of 576 Squadron, Fiskerton, completed the last five of her hundred ops in the hands of F/Lt Stuart B. Simpson and crew on food-dropping sorties over Holland, operation Manna, signified on the side by sacks instead of bombs. The trips were officially credited as ops because of the*

truce with the Germans being of such a doubtful nature. The insignia include a DFC won by a pilot, a swastika for a confirmed fighter kill by her gunners, and a parachute-mine for a 'gardening' sortie. Removal of the exhaust shrouds dates the photograph as immediately after V-E Day.

Phantom of the Ruhr, *BIII*, EE139
*BQ-B, of 550 Squadron, North Killing-
holme, completed her century on a daylight
trip to Le Havre, September 5, 1944,
with F/Lt Joe Hutcheson driving.*

*Beginning her career with 100
Squadron (from which 550 formed) at
Waltham in May 1943, she ultimately
logged 121 trips before being sent to a
conversion unit, surviving the war, only
to be scrapped in January 1946 without
ceremony.*

*Forward of the insignia is the mustard-
coloured gas detection patch as used by
1 Group and which appeared on both
sides of the nose.*

*F/Lt Jack Playford, RCAF, of 100
Squadron, Waltham, in the cockpit of
his BIII, ND458 HW-A, Able Mabel,
after completing her 121st operation
(119 are actually shown here). He had
taken Mabel to her century on February
1, 1945, a trip to Ludwigshaven, and
on her last bombing op to Berchtesgaden
on April 25. With a Manna trip on
May 7, flown by W/O Paul S. Tarry
and crew, she finally logged 132 ops,
before being transferred to the Bomber
Command Instructors' School. This
worthy veteran was finally laid to rest
in 1947.*

*The 100th bomb goes on ND709 F2-J
(top right), a BIII of 635 Squadron,
Downham Market after an op on
Chemnitz, February 14/15, 1945.
Delivered in early 1944, she survived
until August 1947, serving at a number
of conversion units after withdrawal
from squadron use. She is believed to
have been Path Finder Force's only
century-maker.*

*F/O George Blackler of 550 Squadron,
North Killingholme, poses (above) in the
cockpit of The Vulture Strikes, BIII,
PA995 BQ-V, after completing his own
tour of 37 ops (27 of them in this machine)
and the kite's 100th sortie, with a trip to
Chemnitz March 5/6, 1945.*

*Beginning operations in May 1944,
she failed to return from Dessau, March
11, 1945, only a matter of weeks before
the war's end.*

There was great rivalry at Skellingthorpe in the summer of 1944 when both squadrons using the base, Nos. 50 and 61, each had an aircraft nearing its 'century'. Which would win, BI, ED588 VN-G or BIII, ED860 QR-N? It was to be a close race between their regular crews, won in the end by F/Lt Basil Turner and crew taking 'N-Nan' to Vitry-la-Francois on the night of June 27/28. 'G-George's' turn came a week

later, F/Lt Bill Enoch and crew doing a daylight trip to St Leu D'Esserent on July 4. Unfortunately, 'G-George' failed to return with another crew from Konigsberg on the night of August 29/30, 1944, her 128th op. Almost as if bemoaning the loss of her old friend, 'N-Nan', who had by then done 129, spent the whole of September off ops, presumably on major overhaul. She returned to service in October, doing one more op

to bring her total to 130, but on the night of October 28/29, she refused to become airborne on take-off for Bergen, and had to be written off, fortunately without loss of life. Both aircraft achieved over 1,000 hours of flying in a combined total of 36 months of operational use. Not too bad for machines designed for a life expectancy of a mere 40 hours !

A proud bunch of air and ground crew smile for the camera as the 107th bomb is painted on ND578 KM-Y of 44 (Rhodesian) Squadron at Spilsby in January 1945. A BIII, she entered service in February 1944, completed 123 operational trips in the fourteen months to April 1945 and soldiered on until after Operation 'Dodge' in which she took part, being finally retired late in 1945. F/Lt L. W. Hayler and crew did 34 ops in Y-Yorker and had the honour of taking her on her 100th – to Karlsruhe on the night of February 2/3, 1945. The card in the cockpit side-window was a permanent fixture, 'borrowed' by her crew from London Zoo. It read: 'These animals are dangerous.'

'Mother of them all', Bomber Command's top-scoring 'heavy' with 140 trips. G/Capt Sheen, 'Station Master' of Elsham Wolds, paints a DSO on 576 Squadron's veteran BIII, ED888, UL-M² after completing 102 ops. Centre is P/O Jimmy Griffiths who did 30 trips in her and took her up to 99, taking with him on that trip P/O J. B. 'Tinkle' Bell as second dickey and showing not only how she handled but also how to destroy a Ju88 (the crew's second confirmed fighter). The old girl was handed over to Bell and it fell to him and his crew on their first op to

take her on her 100th – to Wizernes, July 20, 1944. ED888 started her operational career with 103 Squadron in May 1943, completing 54 sorties before being taken over by 576 Squadron on its formation from a flight of 103 and 101 Squadrons in November. After 77 ops with 576, she returned to 103 for a further nine trips before retirement, her last being to Cologne on Christmas Eve 1944, captained by F/O S. L. Saxe, RCAF. She was tragically scrapped without thought in January 1947 after languishing at an MU for over two years.

WINGS FOR VICTORY

WINGS FOR VICTORY *Lancs played their part in the Wings for Victory savings campaigns and several cities up and down the country had one on display. A new machine cost some £40,000 and many millions of pounds were raised.*

Here are three examples: London (facing page, upper) had 'O-Orange' of 207 Squadron (BI, L7580 EM-O) in Trafalgar Square; Leeds had (facing page, lower) 'P-Peter' of 97 (Straits Settlements) Squadron (BI, R5552 OF-P). *Both were operational veterans, the former having completed 27, the latter 47 sorties.*

It was appropriate that Manchester should have a Lanc for their Wings for Victory effort in March 1943. Above is ED749, *a brand new BI and destined to survive a collision with a German fighter coming back from Stuttgart in the early hours of February 21, 1944, losing six feet of her port wing as well as having the dorsal turret shattered.*

This Lanc, BIII ED930 *(below left), is seen in the Australian outback while on a fund-raising tour of Australasia. For most Aussies, it was their first sight of the aircraft on which so many of their fellow-countrymen were serving, 12,000 miles away. Christened* Queenie, *she flew out from Prestwick in May 1943, in the capable hands of F/Lt Peter Isaacson and his regular crew (the first all-Australian Lanc crew to complete a tour of operations).*

Australia was reached via Canada, the USA, and the Pacific in 72 hours flying. She toured most of Australia and New Zealand and in one day alone helped to raise £17,480. Eventually, she became the pattern aircraft for Lancaster production in Australia, which, as it turned out, was never proceeded with.

In this photograph Queenie *bears South East Asia style roundels. The camouflage later gave way to a natural metal finish and the serial became A-66-1.*

MERCY MISSIONS

MERCY MISSIONS *The last bombing operations by Lancs were the destruction by day of Hitler's 'Eagles Nest' at Berchtesgaden on April 25, 1945, and oil storage depots at Vallo (Norway) the same night, but the war was not yet over for the crews. Only four days later they were called in again – to drop, not bombs, but food.*

With communications in Europe at a standstill, and the Germans on the brink of defeat, thousands of Dutch people were left without supplies of food and in a desperate plight. Operation 'Manna' swung into action and, in the space of ten days, Lancasters dropped over 6,500 tons of food from specially designed bomb bay panniers. Although a truce was arranged with the Germans to allow the food-drop to take place, several Lancs were fired on and each aircraft flew fully-crewed and armed 'just in case'.

A 3 Group Squadron, No. 115, carried out the food-dropping trials, the technique being perfected by Major R. P. Martin of the South African Air Force, one of 115's Flight Commanders, and one of several South Africans serving with Bomber Command.

Many air and ground crews contributed their own rations of cigarettes and chocolates for the actual operation, preparations for which went on day and night.

A Mildenhall-based 15 Squadron Lanc unloads its groceries over Holland. NX561, a BI (BVII Interim) flown by F/O C. Hall and crew over The Hague early in May 1945.

ONLY TWO HOURS FROM HOME SWEET HOME *The next and most urgent task was the repatriation of British Prisoners of War, and by V-E Day, May 8, Operation 'Exodus' was well under way. Each Lanc carried 25 passengers, many of whom were a pathetic sight after up to six years in captivity, dressed in any old clothes they could get hold of. In 26 days, 74,000 ex-PoWs were brought home from Brussels and Juvincourt.*

This 149 (East India) Squadron Lanc was, only a few days before, leading a G-H 'vic' on a daylight raid. Now, covered in goodwill messages, she stands at Juvincourt ready to receive her expectant, excited load of passengers, all longing for their first sight of 'Blighty' again and sharing a welcome cigarette with the aircrew before take-off. A lot of the PoWs had themselves been shot down while on Lancs and how they relished their ride!

Included in the repatriation were many Belgian, Dutch and French refugees and this rather bewildered little group waits to board a 514 Squadron Lancaster at Waterbeach on May 17, 1945, some seeing their homeland for the first time in six years.

THE FINAL ACT *for many squadrons before disbanding for good, following Japan's capitulation, was the repatriation of troops from Italy – Operation 'Dodge', in which approximately 100,000 men were ferried home. Many were former 'Desert Rats' of the famous 8th Army who had served throughout the North African campaign, then in the Allied push through Italy, some having been away for nearly five years and who were now only a seven-hour flight from home.*

The scene at Bari in September 1945 as a line of Lancs, now with post-war underwing serials, await their loads of 24 passengers with kit.

FIELD FULL OF LANCS *At one stage of Operation 'Dodge', which lasted from late August until early 1946 over 100 Lancs were stranded in Italy for nearly two months, due to bad weather. Here at Pomigliano they stand stretching almost as far as the eye can see, on roughly-laid metal hardstandings, unable to use the water-logged taxi-tracks or runway.*

Through the summer of 1945 the wartime Squadrons had been maintained in preparation for 'Tiger Force' to carry on the fight against Japan, but following the Atom Bomb and Japan's early surrender, there was a rapid run-down and the end is near for many of the squadrons and the Lancs depicted here.

LANCS FROM CANADA

BRAND NEW *Fresh off the Victory Aircraft production line and awaiting delivery to Britain for use by the Canadian squadrons based in the North East. All three turret positions are faired over for the delivery flights via Prestwick, the turrets being fitted on arrival at maintenance units. These Lancs are from an early Canadian production batch, having the 'needle-blade' props. Altogether 430 Lancs were produced in Canada of which 320 were delivered to the UK between September 1943 and August 1945. Clearly visible in this photograph are the bulged bomb doors – a requirement of 6 Group for carrying 8,000lb bombs.*

OFF HOME *With the war in Europe over, the Canadian squadrons soon returned home to prepare for Tiger Force, and the battle against Japan. These scenes are at Middleton St George on the last day of May 1945 as (left) the Lancs of 428 'Ghost' Squadron are lined up for a ceremonial send-off and (below) the British ground crews wave a sentimental goodbye and good luck to a Canadian crew as the throttles are opened up for the homeward journey via the Azores. Amongst the well-wishers were the C-in-C 'Bomber' Harris and 'Black' McEwen, OC of 6 Group.*

BACK HOME *a Canadian Flying Officer proudly points out his Lanc's part in winning the war – 72 ops! BX* KB760 *NA-P of the 'Ghost' Squadron.*

GRAVEYARDS

WAR SURPLUS *The war is over. Almost overnight the squadrons disband and hundreds of Lancs are put out to grass. Some were scrapped almost immediately while others were to languish in fields for several years, awaiting their fate.*

However, many new machines were stored at maintenance units for the Lanc continued in front-line service *with Bomber Command until superseded by the Lincoln in 1947/9, while they were to fly with Coastal Command until October 1956.*

Above is a line-up of veterans at Silloth MU.

THEIR WINGS CLIPPED *Scenes at Malton, Ontario (below and facing page, upper), as brand new Lancs stand cold and unwanted, surplus to requirements, the war in Europe over and Tiger Force disbanded as they were being completed. These are Lancs of a later production batch, with Martin mid-upper turrets and 'paddle-blade' props.*

REPRIEVE *The end of the war did not mean the end of life for the Lancaster. The return of American aircraft under the terms of Lease Lend led to a shortage of reconnaissance and rescue aircraft and it fell to the Lanc to fulfil these roles as a stop-gap measure until newer types* were available.

As the political situation in the early post-war years worsened, Canada in particular had a vast coastline to patrol. Numbers of Mark Xs, new machines and veterans alike, were taken from storage and converted – some remaining in service with the RCAF until 1964.

Rabbit's Stew, *still bearing the mementoes of its wartime service, is prepared for conversion at the Malton, Ontario, plant of A. V. Roe, Canada in 1952.*

AIRFIELDS - THEN AND NOW

AIRFIELDS - THEN AND NOW

Within a year of the cessation of hostilities, the majority of wartime bomber bases were run down and abandoned. Most reverted to farmland and the farmers from whom the land was requisitioned. Officially, they were classified as 'Agricultural Category 4', which meant they could be ploughed up and farmed, providing runways, pipes and cables were left intact.

Squatters were quick to move in and farmers also found a ready use for the hangars and numerous Nissen huts for storing farm implements and the like.

Today, a quarter of a century later, even the runways and dispersals on many airfields have disappeared, having been ripped up for such use as underlays on new motorways. Most of the huts have long since gone and even the black hangars at some bases have been pulled down.

An aerial view of Graveley (above) in 1944 showing the mass of huts and roads. The area occupied by a typical airfield was some 600 acres.

The Watch Office at Graveley (top) as viewed in 1967.
The sole remaining hangar at Gransden Lodge (above) in 1967.
Only seven years after the war, crew huts at Kirmington (left) reduced to rubble.

137

FIDO *demonstration at Fiskerton, 1944 for 49 Squadron crews. This view (above) illustrates to advantage the layout of an airfield built during the war, with black T2 hangars in sharp contrast to the green of the surrounding farmland.*

Painting of a Lanc on the wall of a hut before demolition at Fiskerton in 1961.

By Ermine Street to yesterday

Don Charlwood

Since the end of the war many former Lancaster men have felt a compulsive urge to revisit the airfields from whence they flew on operations.

For those living in Great Britain it is at most no more than a few hours' drive, or a slight detour when on the way to the coast with their families.

However, for the men from the Commonwealth it is more difficult. Some are lucky in being sent to the UK by their company, while others have to save up for years to make the pilgrimage. For all it is a highly emotional experience.

One who returned is Don Charlwood, an Australian from Victoria. His book *No Moon Tonight*, published in 1956, in which he describes his experiences with the RAF, is a classic. The following account was written after a visit to his old haunts in 1958.

Before we began our journey I rang up a number in Cleethorpes. Even after fifteen years, it came easily to my tongue. The voice that had welcomed me then, welcomed me now, nor had the voice changed, although the speaker was past her eighty-sixth year. I remembered going to her home on nights when Bomber Command operations had been cancelled and all Lincolnshire lay under low cloud.

The afternoon was wet and windy, but by five the sky had cleared and down the long, level road I saw Lincoln Cathedral, pale over its city. I remembered it then in cruciform as it appeared to us when we had set course early for Germany, or on days when we had flown low over Lincolnshire for the joy of flying. Soon an odd shock came to me; for the approach to Brigg was upon us long before I had expected it, before I had convinced myself that this was the land of that other life. Insensibly I withdrew from my family. In fifteen years these hills had become places of the spirit to me, so that I saw them now with numb surprise: the windmill outside Brigg, the flesh wasted from its bones; Gallows Wood, now very green, then bare; Barnetby cross-roads above Barnetby village.

I stopped at the cross-roads, the feeling on me that if these hills were real, then hereabouts there must yet be men who had known those days. Signposts pointed east to Grimsby, south to Barnetby, north to Elsham. I felt drawn by the Elsham road, but resolved to come back to it alone. I turned north into the village, descending to the railway that had brought us to squadron life in the autumn of 1942 and had taken us away again. The war had come and the war had gone and there was little change there. We climbed the other side of the valley to a disused Saxon church, sunken in its graveyard, crudely buttressed by men a thousand years dead.

I had once known it well. From its mounded earth it had been possible to see aircraft lift off the Elsham runways, three or four miles away. But now I could see nothing, could only hear the thin whistle of a train in the valley, the train we had caught, no doubt, when departing for leave in London.

Before dark we reached Cleethorpes. When dinner was served I sat again at the head of the table I had known then, the same gracious matriarch before me. I looked at my family with the same faint surprise that had come to me in the wolds two hours before.

"Tomorrow," I said, "I must go to Elsham."

The afternoon was bleak and wet, a day of winter rather than summer. Alone on the Brigg road I passed the gaunt ribs of Kirmington aerodrome, which had once been our satellite. Ahead rose the highest part of the wolds where we had lived.

I had always vowed that if I returned to England, I would walk from Barnetby to Elsham as we had done before. Clearly I would have to break my vow. The rain was steady, my time limited, and the way was incredibly long. As I drove the three miles to the aerodrome, I marvelled that often I had walked this way to Barnetby and back again and then had flown all night. Invariably, it seemed, the weather had been cold, or rain had blown from the North Sea. The trees, the hedges, the fields were miraculously unchanged; I saw a misshapen oak whose arms I had often watched against searchlight beams, a symbol, I had thought then, of the two lives we were living simultaneously.

I turned left to the top of the wolds and came soon to two brick pillars from which the cement was peeling. Here, in 1942, had been our gate. Close by, the guard-house and the sick-quarters were in ruins, heaps of rubble overgrown with nettles. I kept my eyes turned away still from the aerodrome and the main group of buildings, fearing that all sign of them would be gone. But when I looked, I saw that the main hangar, the watch-office and the water-tower were there still, squat under the rainy sky. Nearer, the dispersal points were empty and the runways were infested with weeds.

I remembered leaving that distant mess one April day in 1943. We had been sitting together as a crew for the last time, our tour over. Our jubilation had drained away, for it seemed incredible that we who had lived so closely should now go our separate ways. I remember nothing of our conversation, but I recall that we were eating bacon and eggs, not by right, but as a last favour to an emeritus crew. Bacon and eggs were the privilege of the men about us. In their white sweaters and their flying-boots they dwelt in a realm far removed from our own. We looked on them with understanding and a degree of envy, but also with relief and not a little benevolent patronage. I left the mess first, for I had a train to catch in Barnetby. We exchanged the usual laconic remarks. Outside there was thick fog. The nearer Lancasters waited, noses to air, but the runways and hangars were invisible. The roads of the camp were busy with cars and bicycles and men on foot, everyone preoccupied with the night's operation.

Now the road was empty. Most of the dispersed Nissen huts had gone, but I had the illusion again that in the intact buildings ahead there must yet be men, or at least a sign left for me. Near the administration block I parked the car. From fifty yards the mess still looked inhabited. I walked through the rain and went in at the open door, all at once anticipating the smell of beer and bacon and wet greatcoats, the sound of voices. But down the long room lay ploughs and harrows and bags of superphosphate. The windows were obscure with dust and cobwebs; the cheap lining of the ceiling hung in tatters. I stood very still. Somewhere hens were clucking and rain gurgled off the roof. There were no other sounds at all. Something in the room eluded me; a deafness shut me from messages on the dusty air. I walked quickly into the rain, groping for understanding of our silenced activity, the purpose of all the courage and devotion I had once seen.

A cracked and puddled road led to the operations block, the bombing-trainer, the barber's shop, the main stores and, finally, the flight office. By a piece of irony amusing and obscene, the long building was now a piggery. Dung was raked into piles where once we had held morning parade – as if the curses of vanished crews had been taken literally by some omnipotent being. The pigs were squealing in conference over the hideous dissolution. I walked slowly to the perimeter track. The wind came clean and free across the last earth touched by our wheels.

I reached the car wet and cold. Rain was still falling steadily, but I stood for a long time, casting about again for some sign of all the comradeship and courage that had ennobled this tattered hill. But the woods and the earth were dumb and the rest was a skull, white in the rain. At the gate I felt an urge to write across the decaying columns: 'Here was the home of 103 Squadron, RAF Bomber Command, 1941–45.'

Under the edge of the aerodrome, at the head of a valley there, I came to Elsham village; a solitary, semi-circular village deserted in the rain. Once it had had a priory, but, like the men of Elsham Wolds, the monks had gone and the priory had gone; only a well, it was said, remained. In the porch of the church I found the names of priors and vicars dating to 1220, and of churchwardens whose family names were repeated over the centuries. I went inside, and on the north wall climbed to a high gallery. I had never been in the church, but once – on the Sunday after El Alamein – we had heard its bells, an unaccustomed, joyful sound, rising from this valley. The war then had seemed almost over.

Close under the roof I could hear rain overtaking the gutters. Except for a tin trunk and a chest of drawers the gallery was empty, but with a start I noticed the bust of a bearded man regarding me fixedly from the shadows. I retreated before his gaze, down to the nave and out of the door.

On the list of churchwardens in the porch the name 'Holmes' was several times repeated, once in 1604, as 'Houlmes'. This had been the name of our mid-upper gunner, a native of these parts and one of the finest poachers on this part of the wolds. His escapades, and the meals he had provided for the crew, and the verve with which he had lived had endeared him to all of us.

THE DAMBUSTERS - FACT AND FILM

THE DAM BUSTERS – FACT

No book on the Lancaster would be complete without mention of its most famous exploit – the breaching of the Ruhr dams by 617 Squadron on the night of May 16/17, 1943. Photographs of the weapon and of the aircraft used on the raid are rare, but (left) is shown a close-up of the special mine designed by Barnes Wallis. The belt drive is to the motor which spun the mine before dropping.

W/Cdr Guy Gibson's aircraft, AJ-G, ED932, is seen (below) at Scampton in January 1947 in use at that time with the Station Flight. After the Dams Raid, it continued on operations with 617 Squadron, being used to drop the 12,000lb tallboys, and was finally scrapped without thought or ceremony in July 1947.

THE DAM BUSTERS – FILM

By the time the decision was taken to make the film in 1953, Lancasters were already in short supply, and four Mk.7s had to be taken out of storage and specially modified. The actual mine was still on the secret list and the mock-up bore little resemblance, though the underhang is thought to have been specially accentuated for filming purposes to make it more obvious.

These photographs were taken by two of the crewmen who did the flying for the film, all crews being on Lincolns based at Hemswell.

Memorial erected at Kelstern in honour of 625 Squadron, with remnants of a once-busy operational station in the background.

The people of the Low Countries have many reasons to be grateful to the boys of Bomber Command. This memorial was erected by the Dutch at Dronten, East Pievoland (formerly the Zuider Zee). The prop is off a 12 Squadron Lanc BI, ED357, brought down by a night fighter on the night of June 11/12, 1943, and salvaged by the Royal Netherlands Air Force in 1962. A memorial service is still held here on each V-E Day anniversary.